NATIVE AMERI
MYTHS

NATIVE AMERICAN
MYTHS

STORIES & FOLKLORE FROM THE APACHE TO THE ZUNI

CHRIS McNAB

amber
BOOKS

This edition first published in 2023

Copyright © 2018 Amber Books Ltd

Published by Amber Books Ltd
United House
London N7 9DP
United Kingdom
www.amberbooks.co.uk
Instagram: amberbooksltd
Pinterest: amberbooksltd
Twitter: @amberbooks

All rights reserved. With the exception of quoting brief passages for the purpose of review no part of this publication may be reproduced without prior written permission from the publisher. The information in this book is true and complete to the best of our knowledge. All recommendations are made without any guarantee on the part of the author or publisher, who also disclaim any liability incurred in connection with the use of this data or specific details.

ISBN: 978-1-83886-279-4

Project Editor: Michael Spilling
Designer: Zoe Mellors
Picture Researcher: Terry Forshaw

Printed in United States

CONTENTS

INTRODUCTION 6

1. CREATION AND THE UNIVERSE 8

2. PEOPLE, FAMILY AND CULTURE 42

3. THE NATURAL WORLD 70

4. GHOSTS, SPIRITS AND THE DEAD 100

5. GODS, MONSTERS AND GREAT BEINGS 134

6. HUMANITY - LOVE, LIFE, MORALITY AND DEATH 164

7. WARRIOR RACE 194

BIBLIOGRAPHY 222
INDEX 222

INTRODUCTION

It is a common bias in the West to describe North American history beginning with the European colonial settlements of the 16th century, which laid the foundations of what would become the modern United States and Canada. Yet these events – a mere 400 years of time – are temporally eclipsed by the history of the indigenous peoples, the Native Americans.

Their story, enacted across the vast tracts of North America, stretches back anywhere from 16,000 to 30,000 years ago, at the point when early humans moved across the Bering land bridge (Beringia) from Siberia into north-west North America. Over the subsequent thousands of years, the new arrivals spread from this icy foothold across the whole of the Americas, establishing tribal territories and local identities as they did so.

Below: A Cherokee mother and daughter make pots of clay on the Qualla Reservation, North Carolina, in this 1880s photograph. Native American myths often feature on craftware.

ORAL HISTORY

At the moment the first European colonists stepped ashore in North America, therefore, the Native Americans already had their own long history. But that history, and the cultures developed within it, was not codified and recorded in written texts, but instead told in a vibrant tapestry of oral traditions – collections of myths, legends and narratives passed down across centuries. These are true living histories. Each story would be injected with the drama and interpretation of the storyteller, the twists and turns of plot and character energized for a rapt audience gathered around a crackling campfire. At the same time, the storyteller would adhere faithfully to the core details and structure of the narrative, ensuring its accurate transmission across the ages.

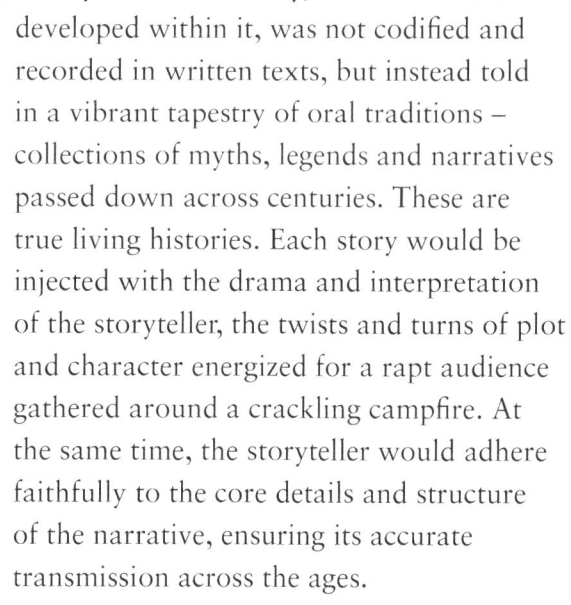

This book brings together a thematically broad collection of myths and legends from across Native American cultures, from the Tlingit peoples of the frozen north to desert-dwelling Apache. Writing such a work, and collecting and selecting the narratives for inclusion, brings an author face to face with worldviews very different to those that prevail today. In the modern urban context, materialism and individualism generally underpin our philosophical outlooks, however much we try to resist them. We can and do practice spirituality, but this tends to be confined to a specific place of worship, or individual acts of devotion, pools of peace in the midst of hurried lives. Furthermore, as the majority of us live in towns and cities, our perspectives on life are figuratively and literally hemmed in by urbanization, nature overlaid by concrete and tarmac.

MAN AND NATURE

Native American mythology, by contrast, is utterly integrated with nature. The myths and legends are bounded only by limitless sky, endless plains, rolling tundra and lush woodlands. Spirits abound, from lonely ghosts up to great Sky Gods and epic monsters, ever present alongside the people who attempt to interact and negotiate with them. The world of humans and nature is seamless and interconnected, animals, plants, even rocks sharing in narratives as equal characters. All aspects of nature are engaged in the physical act of survival and in the diurnal, seasonal and annual rhythms of life. They thus have to find a communicative balance with one another, and the myths and legends told by the Native Americans are often about how that balance is achieved, disrupted or restored.

Yet as we shall see throughout this book, despite their lofty sense of nature and the spirit world, most of the myths and legends are squarely down to earth when it comes to humanity. Many central characters are morally ambiguous, neither fully good nor fully evil, as in life. This is, I would argue, part of the reason why Native American myths are so compelling to a modern readership. They are relevant because they connect with what it means to be human. We can identify with the characters, and therefore find answers to our own life questions.

Above: This Kiowa shield cover is decorated with a turtle, a thunderbird, stars and the Milky Way.

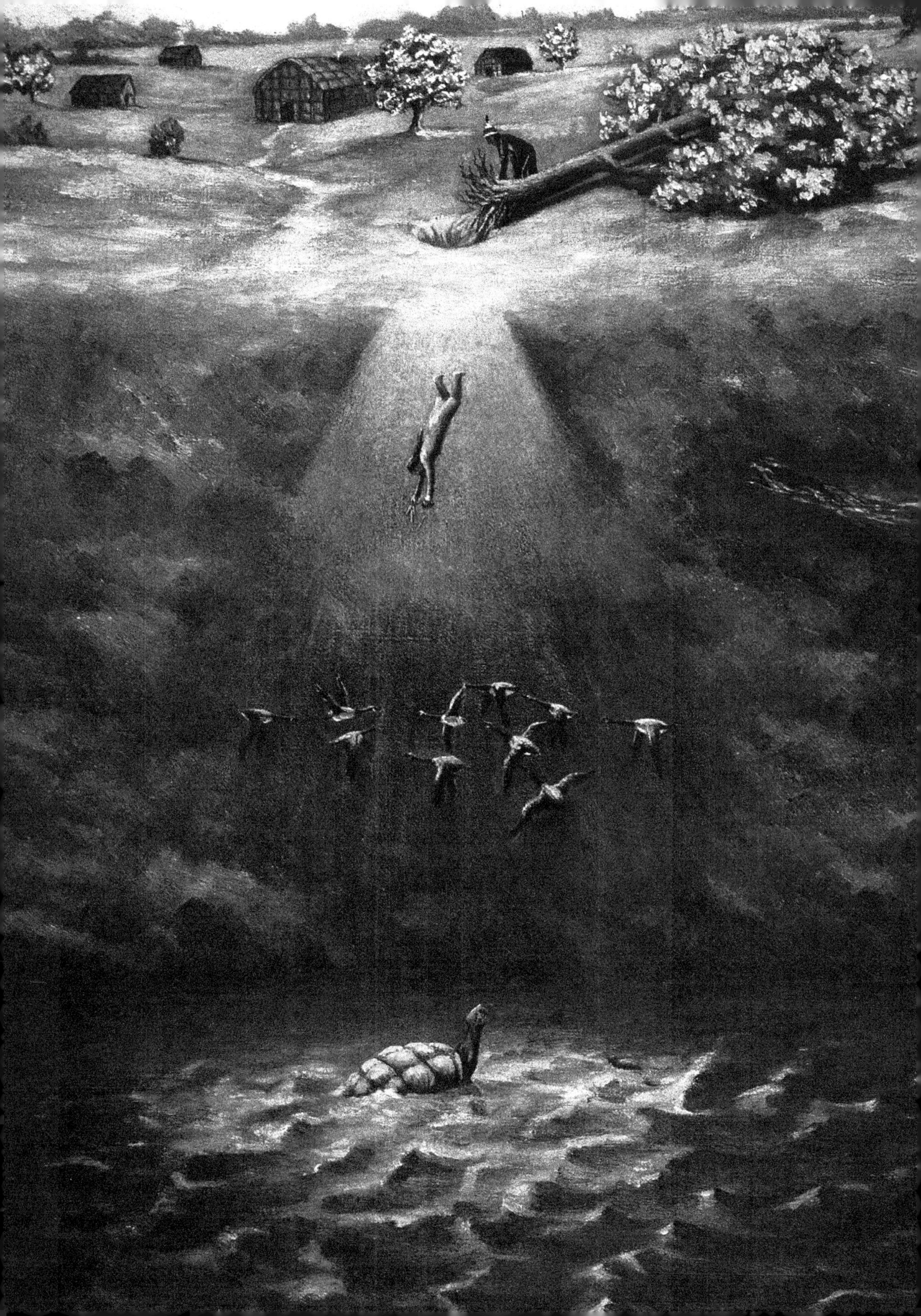

CREATION AND THE UNIVERSE

For those of us who are familiar with the biblical tradition of creation, Native American genesis narratives are a step into the unfamiliar. The Judeo-Christian account of the origins of matter and life sees God creating the Earth and all that lives upon it through an act of divine sanction. It is a simple but powerful model, a magnified version of acts of human creativity, like a builder creating a house.

MANY NATIVE American creation accounts do hinge upon a creator being, a figure of universal power who either shapes the world physically or at least guides the direction of its emergence.

THE MASTER OF LIFE (PIMA)
The Pima people of what is now known as southern and central Arizona told of the 'Master of Life'. Like a craftsman at work, this Master of Life literally sculpted all that the Pima saw around them – rocks, canyons, river valleys, the *mesa* tablelands, the

Left: A dreamlike depiction of an Iroquois creation myth by Ernest Smith in 1936. The Sky Woman falls from her realm down to the world below, the giant turtle receiving her and becoming the foundation for the Earth.

Above: A Pima earth lodge, made from wattle and daub with a thick covering of soil. A smoke hole in the centre of the roof would let out the smoke from cooking.

grasses and flowers, plus all the creatures that flew, swam and crawled there. Only once the Earth was shaped and imbued with its flora and fauna did the Master of Life then reflect upon the need for human beings to complete and manage creation. In a loose parallel with the Genesis narrative, the Master of Life decides to make human beings in his own image, although the creative process is highly manual – the Master literally crafting the humans from a ball of clay and baking it in a cosmological kiln.

Yet the process of creating human beings would not be straightforward for the Master of Life, for it was subject to the interference of that most wily of characters, the Coyote. While the Master was out collecting wood, the Coyote took the hardening figure from the kiln and remodelled it in the image of a humble dog. When the Master returned, he took the figure from the kiln and breathed life into it, at which point he was confronted by an animate and barking animal. Sensing the culprit, the Master rebuked the Coyote for his manipulation and started again on his quest to create human beings. This time he formed two figures, distinguished by the biological differences that would enable them to reproduce. Back into the kiln they went, but again the Coyote would not do as he was bid. He told the Master that with his keen nose he could smell the figures burning and that they should be removed immediately. The Master did so, but on inspection it was apparent that they were underdone and had pale skin. Anger raged in him, and once again he rebuked the Coyote. But creation could not be undone, and thus the Master breathed life into the figures anyway. These humans did not belong in the lands created by the Master, so he sent them away to another place, far across the sea, and resumed his work from scratch.

The next attempt was again frustrated by the Coyote, who this time prevented the Master from removing the figures from

THE PROCESS OF CREATING HUMAN BEINGS WOULD NOT BE STRAIGHTFORWARD FOR THE MASTER OF LIFE, FOR IT WAS SUBJECT TO THE INTERFERENCE OF THAT MOST WILY OF CHARACTERS, THE COYOTE.

Below: Petroglyph carvings of animal figures on a rock by the Salt River, Arizona; the Pima lived around Arizona's Gila and Salt rivers.

the kiln when he judged that they were done. The predictable result was that the humans were over-hardened, and this time their skin turned a pure black. Like the pale-skinned humans before them, these humans did not belong in the Master's land either, so after they were given life they too were sent to another distant place across the sea.

And so the Master of Life once more resumed his thwarted quest to produce human beings in his own image, but this time he did not heed the Coyote's trickster voice, removing the figures from the kiln at the perfect moment when they were a golden copper brown. It was these people who would become the Pima Indians, inhabiting an arid corner of the United States.

Although the Master of Life title might suggest an omnipotent and omniscient God, as the narrative unfolds it becomes clear that comparisons between the Judeo-Christian creator god and the Pima divinity are forced and unnatural. The Master of Life, as with so many of the Native American creator figures, has a core human fallibility, only producing the humans he desired on his fourth attempt, having been gullibly swayed previously by the trickster Coyote. In other myths, we are introduced to creator figures who are capricious, mistaken, angry, inefficient and easily misled. These are not deities who transcend the humanity they create, but rather fully participate in the beauty and fallibility of their creations. This is why, at a base level, the Native American creation myths feel so authentic to the people and the landscape in which they were formed. What is also interesting is how the myth accounts for the diversity of races, acknowledging the presence of wider human society beyond the immediate people of the tribal lands.

> IN OTHER MYTHS, WE ARE INTRODUCED TO CREATOR FIGURES WHO ARE CAPRICIOUS, MISTAKEN, ANGRY, INEFFICIENT AND EASILY MISLED.

UNDERWORLD MYTHS

In the first of our creation narratives given above, we see a powerful but flawed figure shaping the world and creatures around him from a blank sheet, bringing form from the formless. Yet in many cases the Native American creation

CREATION AND THE UNIVERSE 13

Left: A modern visual interpretation of the Mandan Native American creation legend; the Mandan people look to ascend the vines that climb up to the world above.

stories explain the existence of the Earth and the tribal world in terms of an emergence from an already present, typically darker place in the continuum of existence. These can perhaps be labelled 'underworld myths', for rather like a Greek Hadean epic, the participants of these narratives undergo a struggle in subterranean darkness in order to emerge into the light of the North American landscape.

The Four Mounds (Jicarilla Apache)

A haunting version of the underworld myth was told by the Jicarilla Apache, who lived for hundreds of years in a broad territory encompassing the Sangre de Cristo Mountains located in southern Colorado, northern New Mexico and parts of the Great Plains. In their genesis story, at the beginning of time humans lived alongside animals in a dark underworld, the Earth above covered with an endless ocean. In this underworld, the

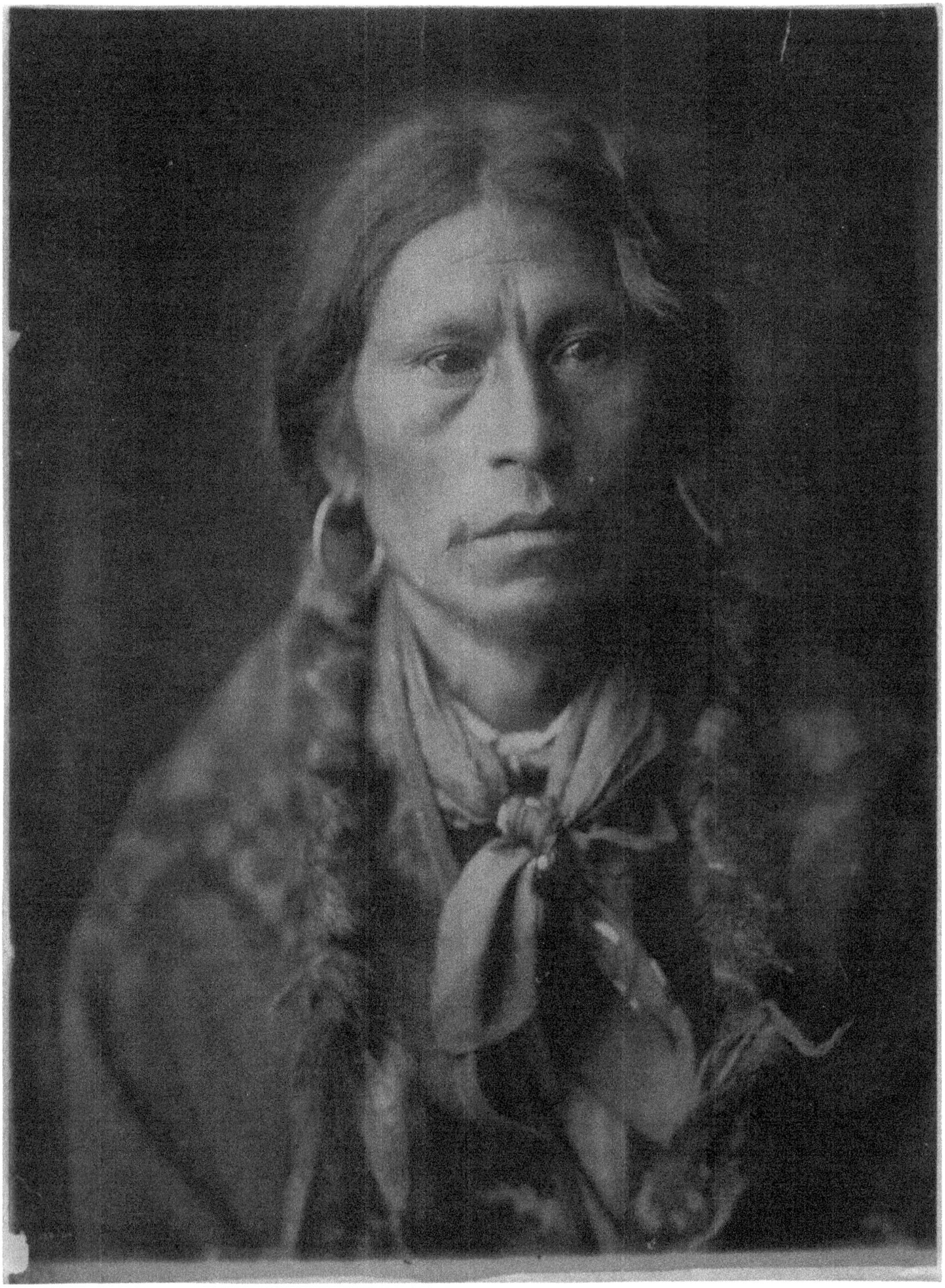

animals had human powers of speech and intelligence, as did the rocks, trees and other features of the natural world. In this place of competing interests, the diurnal creatures – including human beings – wanted more light to illuminate the underworld, while the nocturnal creatures – particularly the bear, owl and panther – preferred to dwell in darkness. To settle matters, the diurnal and nocturnal creatures played a traditional Native American game involving a button and a thimble. They played four times and each time the people won. With each victory, light grew brighter in the east, forcing the nocturnal animals to run away and hide.

The coming of the light provided enough visibility to reveal a hole in the roof of the underworld, through which the denizens of the dark could see the Earth above. The people decided that they would emerge from the darkness onto the Earth, yet it seemed to be far beyond their reach. To get closer to the surface, they constructed four huge mounds, one at each point of the compass, and each planted with specific types of fruit. The eastern mound was festooned with black-coloured fruits and berries; the western mound featured yellow fruits; in the north, there were variegated fruits; and in south were the blue-coloured fruits.

These towering mountains became places where humans foraged and gathered, but still they did not reach the world above. In an attempt to close the gap, the people at first made a series of ladders from feathers, but even the strongest feathers – those of the eagle – were not able to support their weight. The buffalo stepped forward and offered his horns to create a new ladder, one that was indeed strong enough to bear the humans. (As an incidental part of the myth, the buffalo horns were originally straight, but the weight of the humans climbing upon them twisted them into the curled profiles that we see today.) Now the people tied together the Sun and the Moon with spider silk, and let them up into the sky to give greater life to the surface of the Earth. At the same time, four great storms blew up, each

> THESE TOWERING MOUNTAINS BECAME PLACES WHERE HUMANS FORAGED AND GATHERED, BUT STILL THEY DID NOT REACH THE WORLD ABOVE.

Far left: A beautiful portrait of a Jicarilla Apache, the tribe whose traditional lands included parts of present-day Colorado, Oklahoma and New Mexico.

THE CROW DISCOVERED THAT THE EARTH WAS DRY ENOUGH FOR THE HUMANS TO INHABIT, AND SO THE PEOPLE BEGAN TO POPULATE THE LANDS.

corresponding to the placement and colour of the mounds in the underworld. The storms blew with such ferocity that they rolled back the waters, forming oceans in their appropriate places and exposing the land beneath them for the creatures to walk on.

It was the animals that first explored this new world, in so doing acquiring some of their defining physical characteristics. The polecat, for example, took the first step upon the sodden ground, his legs (and therefore those of his species) becoming permanently black from the mud that covered them. The badger, the next to venture up top, also acquired black muddy legs. Both the polecat and the badger returned to the underworld after their adventure, but it was the beaver that stayed at the surface, using his natural skills to build a dam and thereby conserving water for humans to drink.

Eventually the crow, flying far and wide, discovered that the Earth was dry enough for the humans to inhabit, and so the people ascended and began to populate the lands. All the Native American tribes spread out, occupying the places that would become their ancestral territories. Notably, however, the Jicarilla Apaches stayed near to the hole from which they had emerged, circling it three times. When the Ruler of Earth became frustrated by their wanderings, he asked them where they wanted to go and they told him 'The centre of the Earth'. Guided by their desires, the Ruler took them to Taos – located in the north-central desert region of New Mexico – and here they established their home.

Left: A Jicarilla Apache camp, including a traditional tipi. The Jicarilla also lived in 'wickiups', homes made from from reeds and branches bent into an elliptical framework.

Above: Hopi Indian dancers perform a ritual. One particular ritual dance would extend over eight days, and saw the dancers perform while carrying dangerous snakes in their hands and even their mouths.

Ladder Through the Four Worlds (Hopi)

The theme of the creationist ascent from the underworld appears with striking variations in the southwestern corner of the United States. One of the most evocative is that told by the Hopi tribe, who conceived of stratified worlds beneath our own and of a unique journey through them to the surface.

As with the Apache, the Hopi people lived in a dark and oppressive underworld, the lowest of four such places. It was a cave-world, dark, stale and overcrowded, a place of distress and spectral torment. Yet beyond this chthonic imprisonment, there were the higher spirit beings, angelic figures free from such earthly confines. Two of these – the Elder Brother and the Younger Brother – were moved by pity for the human beings suffering in the darkness, and so they punched holes through the three worlds above them and dropped magical seeds down to those below. The seeds implanted themselves in the soil of the cave-world and grew into a strong ladder-like reed-tree, resilient enough to take the weight of the humans. The people, once they discovered the reed-tree through the sense of touch, began to climb it, hoping that they and their families would reach the next world and begin a new life there.

The first people to attain the second world were largely disappointed, as the 'new' world was also underground and still dark and unwelcoming. Nevertheless, they feared that it would soon become overcrowded with those coming up after them, so they shook the reed-tree violently and dislodged those below them, after which they pulled up the tree. The people remaining behind in the first cave-world would need to find their own way out.

Time passed for those in the second world, and as they and their livestock procreated and grew in number, the world became just as crowded as the one that they had left. So once again they took the reed-tree and raised it up, pushing its top through a hole into the third world above them. The people once again made their weary ascent until they reached the third world. Here history repeated itself – those who made it shook the reed-tree to dislodge those following them, and then they too pulled the natural ladder up behind them.

It was in the third world that life finally started to improve for the humans. Here it was lighter than in the worlds below, courtesy of the gift of fire given to them by the Elder Brother and the Younger Brother. Society became more ordered and hierarchical, villages more ordered, and *kivas* – underground chambers used for ritual practices – appeared and came to life with sacred practice. But the period of harmony was not to last. The womenfolk in the third

Below: The interior of a Hopi *kiva* chamber. A small hole dug in the centre of the chamber symbolized the origins of the tribe.

THE SHIELD AND THE MAN WERE THEN HURLED INTO THE EASTERN SKY, BECOMING THE GLOWING SILVERY MOON THAT SHONE DOWN ON THE LANDSCAPE.

world appear to become almost possessed by the desire to dance, drawn in by the ceremonies practised by the local shamans, who dressed as *kachinas* (benign spirits). As the women danced and danced they neglected their family and marital duties, bringing about social chaos as a result.

Once again it was time to escape to the world above, and the reed-tree was erected to allow the people to begin the now-familiar exodus to the higher realm. This time was different, however. When the people climbed up through the hole, they found themselves on the surface of this Earth, emerging from what is today the Grand Canyon. But this Earth was still in a protean form, black and uninhabited and hostile in nature. The chief requirement was additional light, by which the people could find wood to make fire. Here entered the figure of the Spider-Grandmother, who weaved a luminous web that provided some welcome light. But still more was needed. Now

Below: Native American artwork displayed in the Desert View Watchtower, a 21m (70ft) high building constructed on the South Rim of the Grand Canyon in the 1930s to resemble a Pueblo watchtower.

the Coyote, by nature a thief, unwittingly provided the solution as he emerged from the hole, carrying an earthen jar he had stolen. Taking the lid off the jar, all the stars in the skies exploded upwards into the heavens, the sparkling light singeing the Coyote's beard forever black.

However, the light was still not enough to illuminate the world and the solution to the problem lay in the hands of the people. They fashioned a spectacular shield from buffalo hide and cloth, and imbued it with magical powers through sacred incantations and a young man stood atop. Both the shield and the man were then hurled into the eastern sky, becoming the glowing silvery Moon that shone down on the landscape. Now by the light of the Moon they could see the landscape around them, which was still half-formed. Thus they called upon the great Vulture, who flew low over the Earth and created, through the immense downdraft of his wings, the contours of the world with its mountains and valleys. The Elder Brother and Younger Brother then added the rivers that flowed through it.

The Earth was now nearly complete, but it remained cold and it needed a source of heat to warm it for the plants to grow and the people and animals to thrive. Once again, the people made a ceremonial shield, this one highly decorated in strident colours (the first shield had mainly black-and-white patterning), and they decorated it with bright features, cornhusks and an abalone shell placed in the centre. Again, a young man stood bravely on top of the shield as it was swung faster and faster in an expanding arc, and then it was released high into the sky, descending over the eastern horizon. After a period of time, the shield and the man arose from the east, blazing bright as the new Sun. The creation was now complete, and the Hopi Indians settled down to their life on the Colorado Plateau, their journey from the underworld finally behind them.

Above: A buffalo hide *kachina* mask; the *kachina* are spirit beings of the Pueblo people, and wearing an appropriate mask during a specific ritual allowed them to become manifest.

SPIDER-GRANDMOTHER

The Spider-Grandmother, or Spider-Woman, is a powerful and recurrent figure in the mythologies of the American Southwest. She is intimately connected with the act of creation, the webs that she spins often creating the physical fabric of the world, including the formation of solid ground or the bringing of light. The web also represents the interconnectivity of all things, the strands binding nature together in a seamless whole. There is also the sense in which the Spider-Grandmother can act as a guide to the youthful or vulnerable, and as a protector over a tribe. For example, in one Hopi myth the Spider-Grandmother escorts a young man to the realm of the Snake People, guiding him through various and often frightening trials in his quest to discover a beautiful maiden. Eventually he finds himself wrestling one particularly fearsome snake, which the Spider-Grandmother reassures him is actually the maiden. His persistence and the Spider-Grandmother's advice eventually pays off – he purges the anger from the snake, who eventually turns into a beautiful girl.

Left: An illustration of the Spider-Grandmother – referred to as the 'wisdom keeper' – dispensing magical objects to her followers.

ANIMAL NARRATIVES

One particularly sharp contrast between Native American creation myths and those of the Judeo-Christian tradition is the role that mythical animals play in making the world and the people within it. Sometimes the animal's creative act is incidental, the unintended consequence of an act of trickery, theft or inquisitiveness. Other times the act is brave and selfless, often in a moment of interaction with heavenly beings. But what is apparent from all narratives is how the Native Americans see animal life as indivisible from both the act of creation and also the spiritual identity of humanity itself. Humans and animals do not occupy separate realms in this world, but instead participate in one vast and interactive spiritual enterprise. Essentially this is a pantheistic vision, all of existence united through inherent divine qualities.

The Turtle and the Twins (Seneca)

During the 1880s, American translator and folklorist Jeremiah Curtin created one of the most invaluable repositories of Native American mythology when he collected hours of oral traditions from the Seneca people, who at that time were living on the Cattaraugus reservation in New York State. One of the advantages Curtin had was fluency in the Seneca language, but thankfully for the English-speaking world some of the narratives he collected were translated in the early 20th century by I.W.B. Hewitt, which were then presented in the *Report of the Bureau of American Ethnology*.

What follows is one of those narratives, fascinating not only for the temporary but critical role played by the turtle in the creation story, but also for giving us an insight into the creation stories from one of the largest of the five tribes of the Iroquois Confederacy. To preserve as much of the original language and to provide an insight into the Seneca narrators, the 1918 translation is given in full and unedited:

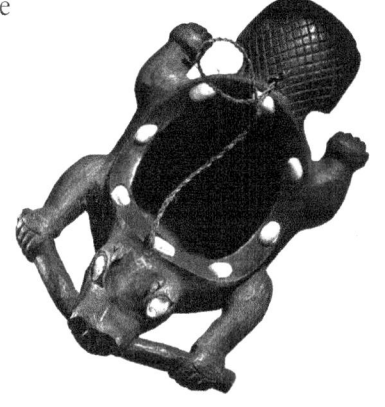

Above: A wooden dish carved into the shape of a swimming beaver. Beavers represent a variety of characteristics in Native American culture, including stubbornness, hard work and heroism.

'A long time ago human beings lived high up in what is now called heaven. They had a great and illustrious chief. It so happened that this chief's daughter was taken very ill with a strange affliction. All the people were very anxious as to the outcome of her illness. Every known remedy was tried in an attempt to cure her, but none had any effect.

'Near the lodge of this chief stood a great tree, which every year bore corn that was used for food. One of the friends of the chief had a dream in which he was advised to tell the chief that in order to cure his daughter he must lay her beside this tree, and that he must have the tree dug up. This advice was carried out to the letter. While the people were at work and

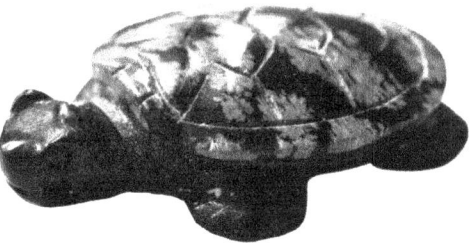

Above: A beautiful representation of the turtle from Zuni Indians, carved from snowflake obsidian stone. Turtles feature in many Native American creation myths.

the young woman lay there, a young man came along. He was very angry and said: "It is not at all right to destroy this tree. Its fruit is all that we have to live on." With this remark he gave the young woman who lay there ill a shove with his foot, causing her to fall into the hole that had been dug.

'Now, that hole opened into this world, which was then all water on which floated waterfowl of many kinds. There was no land at that time. It came to pass that as these waterfowl saw the young woman falling they shouted, "Let us receive her," whereupon they, or at least some of them, joined their bodies together, and the young woman fell on this platform of bodies. When the waterfowl grew weary they asked, "Who will volunteer to care for this woman?" The great Turtle then took her, and when he got tired of holding her, he in turn asked who would take his place. At last the question arose as to what they should do to provide the woman with a permanent resting place in this world. Finally it was decided to prepare the Earth on which she would live in the future.

'To do this it was determined that soil from the bottom of the primal sea should be brought up and placed on the broad, firm carapace of the Turtle, where it would increase in size to such an extent that it would accommodate all the creatures that should be produced thereafter. After much discussion the toad was finally persuaded to dive to the bottom of the waters in search of soil. Bravely

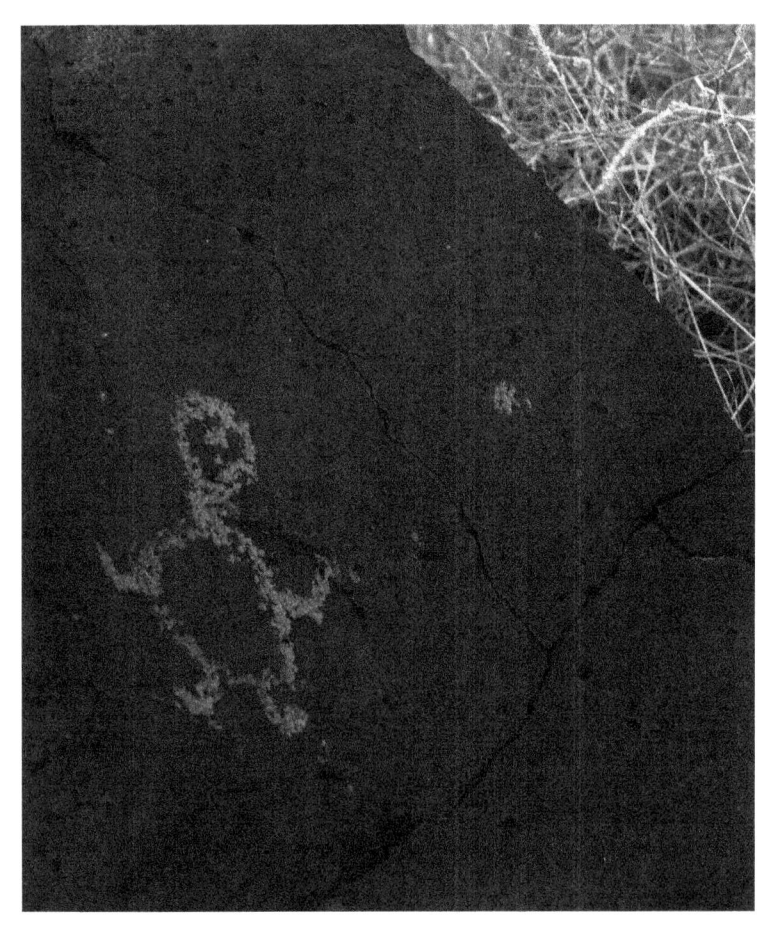

Below: An ancient Native American petroglyph of a turtle. Such was the status of the turtle that some Indian tribes referred to North America as 'Turtle Island'.

making the attempt, he succeeded in bringing up soil from the depths of the sea. This was carefully spread over the carapace of the Turtle, and at once both began to grow in size and depth.

'After the young woman recovered from the illness from which she suffered when she was cast down from the upper world, she built herself a shelter in which she lived quite contentedly. In the course of time she brought forth a baby girl who grew rapidly in size and intelligence. When the daughter had grown to young womanhood, the mother and she were accustomed to go out to dig wild potatoes. Her mother had said to her that in doing this she must face the West at all times. Before long the young daughter gave signs that she was about to become a mother. Her mother reproved her, saying that she had violated the injunction not to face the east, as her condition showed that she had faced the wrong way while digging potatoes. It is said that the breath of the West Wind had entered her person, causing conception. When the days of her delivery were at hand, she overheard twins within her body in a hot debate as to which should be born first and as to the proper place of exit, one declaring that he was going to emerge through the armpit of his mother, the other saying that he would emerge in the natural way. The first one born, who was of a reddish color, was called Othagwenda; that is, Flint. The other, who was light in color, was called Djuskaha; that is, the Little Sprout.

'The Grandmother of the twins liked Djuskaha and hated the other, so they cast Othagwenda into a hollow tree some distance from the lodge. The boy that remained in the lodge grew very rapidly, and soon was able to make himself bows and arrows and to go out to hunt. For several days he returned home without his bow and arrows. At last he was asked

Above: A horned toad figure etched into a shell with acid, the image formed by a Southwestern Native American artist around 700–900 AD.

IT IS SAID THAT THE BREATH OF THE WEST WIND HAD ENTERED HER PERSON, CAUSING CONCEPTION.

why he had to have a new bow and arrows every morning. He replied that there was a young boy in a hollow tree in the neighbourhood who used them. The Grandmother inquired where the tree stood and he told her, whereupon they went there and brought the other boy home again.

'When the boys had grown to man's estate, they decided that it was necessary for them to increase the size of their island, so they agreed to start out together, afterward separating to create forests and lakes and other things. They parted as agreed, Othagwenda going westward and Djuskaha eastward. In the course of time, on returning they met in their shelter or lodge at night, then agreeing to go the next day to see what each had made. First they went west to see what Othagwenda had made. It was found that he had made the country all rocks and full of ledges, and also a mosquito that was very large. Djuskaha asked the mosquito to run in order that he might see whether the insect could fight. The mosquito ran, and sticking his bill through a sapling he fell, at which Djuskaha said, "That will not be right, for you would kill the people who are about to come." So seizing him, he rubbed him down in his hands, causing him to become very small; then he blew on the mosquito, whereupon he flew away. He also modified some of the other animals that his brother had made.

'After returning to their lodge, they agreed to go the next day to see what Djuskaha had fashioned. On visiting the east the next day, they found that Djuskaha had made a large number of animals which were so fat that they could hardly move; that he had made the sugar-maple trees to drop syrup; that he had made the sycamore tree to bear fine fruit; that the rivers were so formed that half the water flowed upstream and the other half downstream. Then the reddish-colored brother, Othagwenda, was greatly displeased with what his brother had made, saying that the people who were about to come would live too easily and be too happy. So he shook violently the various animals – the bears, deer and turkeys – causing

> HE SHOOK VIOLENTLY THE VARIOUS ANIMALS — THE BEARS, DEER AND TURKEYS — CAUSING THEM TO BECOME SMALL.

them to become small at once, a characteristic which attached itself to their descendants. He also caused the sugar-maple to drop sweetened water only, and the fruit of the sycamore to become small and useless; and lastly he caused the water of the rivers to flow in only one direction, because the original plan would make it too easy for the human beings who were about to come to navigate the streams. The inspection of each other's work resulted in a deadly disagreement between the brothers, who finally came to blows, and Othagwenda was killed in the fierce struggle.'

This creation myth is fascinating on many levels. Although the descendants of the Great Chief have heavenly origins, they come across as thoroughly human and fallible in their appetites, prejudices and interrelations. Division and disobedience characterize their early society, leading to expulsion, segregation and ultimately the violent murder of Othagwenda. Such precarious relations are common in Native American mythology; when bound within a creation story, they humanize the narrative of how the world came into being. Yet in many ways at the heart of the story is the turtle, who comes to bear the fabric of Earth itself upon his back,

Above: The Seneca chief Red Jacket (c. 1750–1830). Red Jacket was renowned for his oratory and negotiation skills, the latter used particularly in the land settlements after the American Civil War.

Below: A Lakota Indian engages in prayer to the Great Spirit. The man implores the Great Spirit to endow him with wisdom, life and morality, and the vision to see the truth within nature.

the semi-divine humans performing the minor acts of creation upon his supporting frame. To create the structure, however, the turtle needs the assistance of other members of the animal kingdom, and in particular the toad that dives down into the sea to retrieve the mud from which the world's surface is fashioned.

Another interesting animal element of the story is how Djuskaha and Othagwenda play their part in reshaping the animal kingdom, particularly in downsizing the creatures of the world either to make them less lethal to human beings, or to reduce the volume of food they offer, thus making human life more of a trial of survival. This latter part of the narrative would have had a relevance for those Native American tribes who thrived principally by hunter-gatherer activities rather than agriculture; hunting for survival is a difficult and, in nutritional terms, finely balanced effort, so this creation myth would go some way towards explaining the unrelentingly tough nature of this lifestyle.

The Lakota Creation Story

The turtle appears in several Native American creator myths, not least in that of the Lakota, one of the Great Plains people whose lands traditionally straddled North and South Dakota. What is particularly interesting is how one of the themes of this story – that of a great flood as a destructive punishment visited upon mankind – is a common myth, the best-known version of which is the biblical account of Noah and the Flood in Genesis.

The Lakota story begins with a time and a world before the one that we know. This place was populated by races of people, but over time they became corrupted and displeasing to the Great Spirit, the heavenly being that oversaw all of creation. Aggrieved by what he witnessed, the Great Spirit decided to wipe the surface of the Earth clean. He sang four magical rain songs, each one bringing a greater intensity of water down on the world below. In fact, on the fourth song the Earth itself split apart, and the waters underneath the ground rose up to meet those falling from above, creating a monumental global flood that wiped out all creatures except one – *Kangi*, the crow.

Kangi pleaded with the Great Spirit to give him a new home and somewhere dry to rest above the waters. The Great Spirit relented and reached into a pipe bag that contained specimens of all the world's animals and birds. He drew out four semi-aquatic creatures – a loon (a species of North American diving bird), an otter, a beaver and a turtle. To each he gave the task of diving down to the bottom of the water to retrieve enough mud to form dry land on the surface. For the loon, the otter and the beaver, the challenge proved too much – they could not propel themselves deep enough to reach the seafloor. The turtle, however, swam with great persistence, submerging itself for so long that even the Great Spirit assumed that it had drowned. Yet eventually it broke the surface, carrying with it large amounts of mud between its feet and within its shell. The Great Spirit took the mud and fashioned it into a small patch of land on which the turtle and the crow rested. He then performed a majestic spell of creation, wafting two eagle feathers

THE GREAT SPIRIT TOOK THE MUD AND FASHIONED IT INTO A SMALL PATCH OF LAND ON WHICH THE TURTLE AND THE CROW RESTED.

Below: A turtle being carries the earth upon his back, emphasizing how human beings depend upon nature at the foundations of their existence.

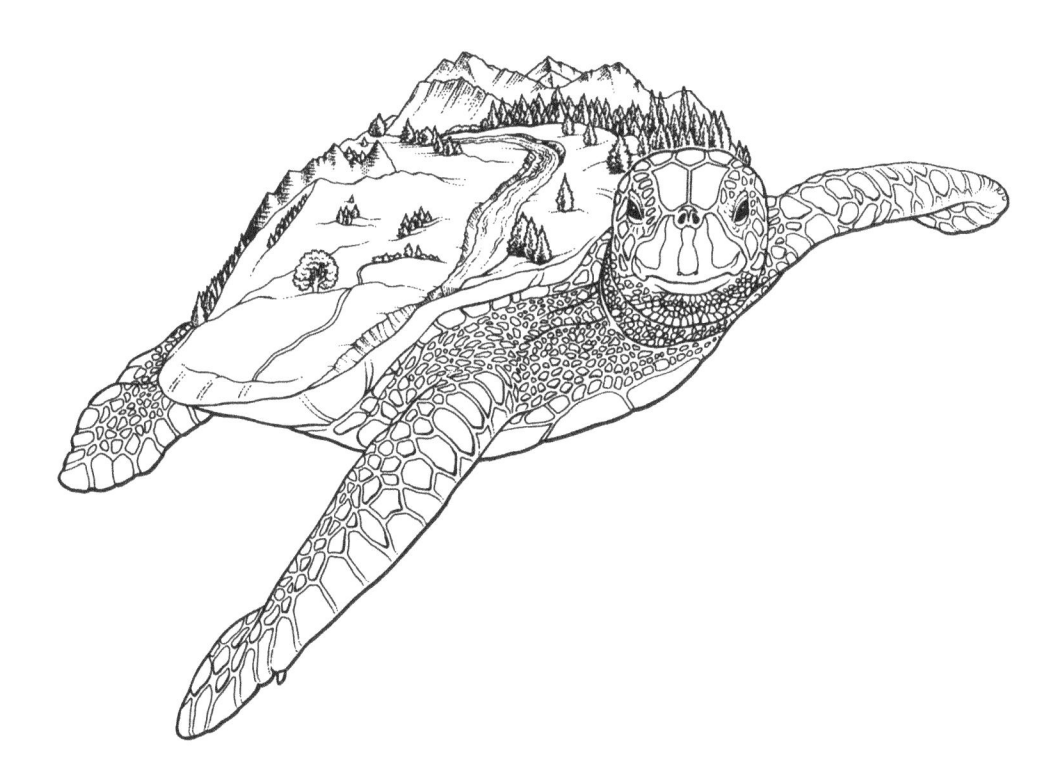

THE DIRECTIONS OF LIFE

DIRECTIONALITY – SPECIFICALLY the points of the compass – is often fundamental to the structure of Native American narratives and to the conception of the world itself. In the Apache creation story given above, north, south, east and west are delineated by the four mounds, each offering different types of fruit to the world, while in the Hopi myth the four holes in the roof of the underworld terminates at the centre – the Grand Canyon – with the heavenly bodies delineating the directions of heat and light. The practical importance of directionality and orientation for the Native Americans is fairly obvious. Not only was the basic rhythm of life dictated by the diurnal swing of the sun from east to west, but the Native Americans also navigated by the stars, which they observed as moving in fixed directions across the night sky, apart from the set position of the polestar.

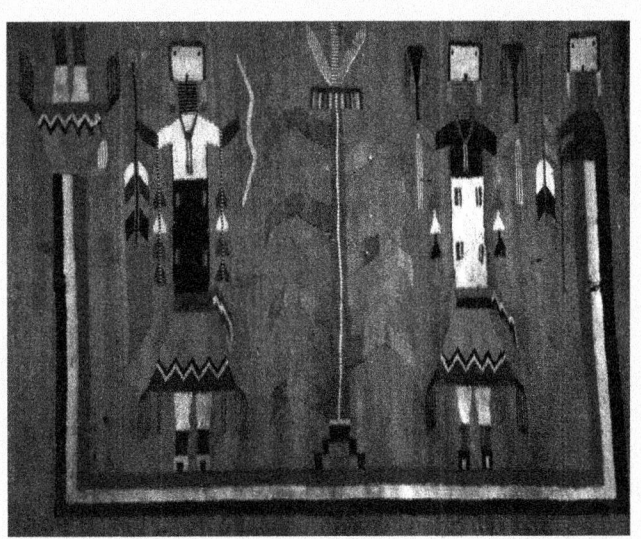

Directionality was also intimately tied to the movements of birds and land animals, such as the annual migration paths of buffalo and other critical sources of food and fur. But the points of the compass were also sacred for demarcating the ancestral lands of many tribes. For example, in the southwest, many of the Native American tribes understood their world to be braced between four sacred mountains located to the north, south, east and west. Here was more than just a sense of territorial limits – within the boundaries was order, harmony and natural balance, whereas outside there was death and chaos. It is also notable how in some tribes, such as the Pueblo and Navajo, for example, the compass points were given characteristics of their own, such as a colour, a distinctive plant type (as we have seen) or the locus of a particular spirit being. But once again, it is the specific landscape of the tribe that often dictates its sense of directionality. Ethnologists have noted, for example, that among the tribes of the Pacific Northwest the directionality is more tied to contrasts in the landscape, such as the meeting of the land and the sea along the coast.

Left: A Navajo blanket depicts a creation myth scene: two supernatural beings flank a sacred maize plant, their gift to the mortal human beings.

over the land and commanding the Earth to spread to become a vast new world, his tears forming the oceans and waterways. Recognizing the efforts of the turtle, this land was called 'Turtle Continent'. The Great Spirit populated it with many more animals from his magical pipe bag, and also crafted the races of humans from various colours of earth.

The Raven and the Light of the World

Other stories of mud-retrieving creatures abound in Native American mythology, particularly along the eastern territories of North America and among the people of the Great Plains. Across the Native American world, an entire menagerie of creatures are co-opted into the act of world creation, including muskrats, dogs, salmon, crawfish, wolves and buffalo. Often an individual animal makes one particular contribution to the emergence of the material world. In northern Northwest Coast mythology, for example, among the Haida, the trickster raven was the creature responsible for bringing light to the people. In a pitch-black world, an old man living in a house by a river owned a box that contained seemingly infinite boxes inside; inside the very last one was all the light of the universe. The old man jealously guarded the box and refused to open it for the rather parentally deficient reason of not wanting to see his daughter's face – he was afraid to reveal possible ugliness.

The cunning raven hatched a plan and magically shrank himself into the form of a tiny hemlock needle, placing himself in a water vessel from which the daughter unwittingly drank,

Above: 'The Raven and the First Men' – a sculpture carved by Haida artist Bill Reid, at the Museum of Anthropology, Vancouver, British Columbia, Canada.

Left: A Haida wooden rattle carved into the shape of a raven. The raven is both culture hero and trickster, moving between dark and light with ambiguity.

Far right: An ornate Pomo dance costume. The Pomo practised the 'ghost dance', a ritual encouraging the return of the dead and the expulsion of the white man.

thereby taking the raven into her body. From this strange union, the raven was reborn from the daughter as a raven/human child, and this hybrid creature became a grandson to the old man. Over time, the raven persuaded the old man through tears and incessant pleading to open all of the boxes. Finally the last box was opened, revealing the light of the world. Quick as a flash, the raven darted forward and grabbed it, flying out of the house and spreading the light as he went and also revealing the old man's daughter as a girl of great beauty. The eagle, jealous of the light, flew at the raven and tried to seize it. This attack caused some of the light to be scattered, and these fragments of light became the Moon and the stars.

Coyote and Cougar (Pomo)

The vivid tale of the raven shows the birth of light as an act of fortunate opportunism, the wiles of the trickster raven bringing benefit to all mankind. A very different mythological take on the relationship between light and the animal spirits is that told by the Pomo Indians in the story of the Coyote and the Cougar. Both creatures had sons who one day played the game of shinny (an informal type of hockey). Yet this was a game of high stakes, for each side had concealed a dangerous creature near the goals –

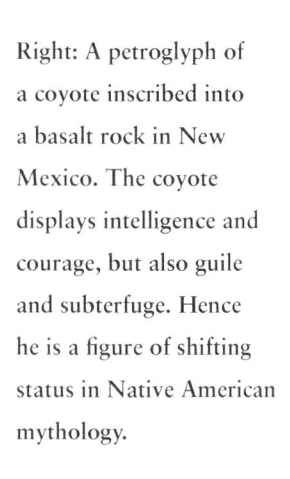

Right: A petroglyph of a coyote inscribed into a basalt rock in New Mexico. The coyote displays intelligence and courage, but also guile and subterfuge. Hence he is a figure of shifting status in Native American mythology.

CREATION AND THE UNIVERSE

on one side was a rattlesnake and on the other a bear. By the end of the game, all but two of Coyote's sons had been killed. The remaining two followed the ball eastwards into a sweat-house. There they were killed by the Sun, who then hung their bodies up on a post to dry out inside the sweat-house, each body held in a leathery bag.

The Coyote did not know the fate of his sons, but a vivid dream told him to go eastwards in his search. He did so, and eventually found the dried-up bodies of his sons in the sweat-house, having to bribe local children with his abalone earrings to make the identification. At night, animals gathered around the bodies with the Coyote, and two mice nibbled through the ropes and cut down his sons. The Coyote, led by his nature,

Below: The Mandan chief Dipäuch sits in his lodge telling an Indian myth of creation to a select group of engrossed warriors.

commanded that the mice be brought to him to eat, but at the last moment he ate two lumps of charcoal instead and spared them.

The animals, accompanied by the Clouds, Rain, Thunder and Stars (the latter the only source of light upon the dark Earth), danced around the post for many hours. Eventually all became weary and were drawn towards sleep. The Coyote, cunning as ever, advised everyone that they should sleep with their heads close together and pointing towards the campfire. While they slept, he crept around and tied their heads together by their hair. He also smothered their bodies in pitch to make it harder for them to pursue him. Seizing the moment, the Coyote grabbed the bodies of his sons and sprinted off with them. The watchman Frog, sat atop the roof of a house, observed the Coyote fleeing from the camp and raised the alarm. The animals around the fire managed to free themselves from their entangled hair and set off in pursuit. The Coyote, meanwhile, was unable to work out which way to flee, such was the impenetrable darkness of the Earth. In defiance, he burst the two bags that held the bodies. At that moment, with a brilliant transformation, one body turned into the Moon and the other into the Sun, flooding the world with light ever after.

This creation myth is a vibrant and, to Western ears, unusual tale, full of moral ambiguity and strange vehicles of creation. What is also implicitly apparent, as in most of the Native American myths, is that these stories come from oral and not written traditions. Oral traditions tend to be more relatable and familiar in their characters and plot twists when compared to literary traditions, not least because they have to be memorable for successive generations to recount them faithfully. Having said this, some Native American creation stories fully embrace a more epic and theological tone to convey the greatness of both the divine spirits and of the world they create. An example of this is the Zuni myth of the Sky-Mother and Sky-Father.

> THE COYOTE, LED BY HIS NATURE, COMMANDED THAT THE MICE BE BROUGHT TO HIM TO EAT, BUT AT THE LAST MOMENT HE ATE TWO LUMPS OF CHARCOAL INSTEAD AND SPARED THEM.

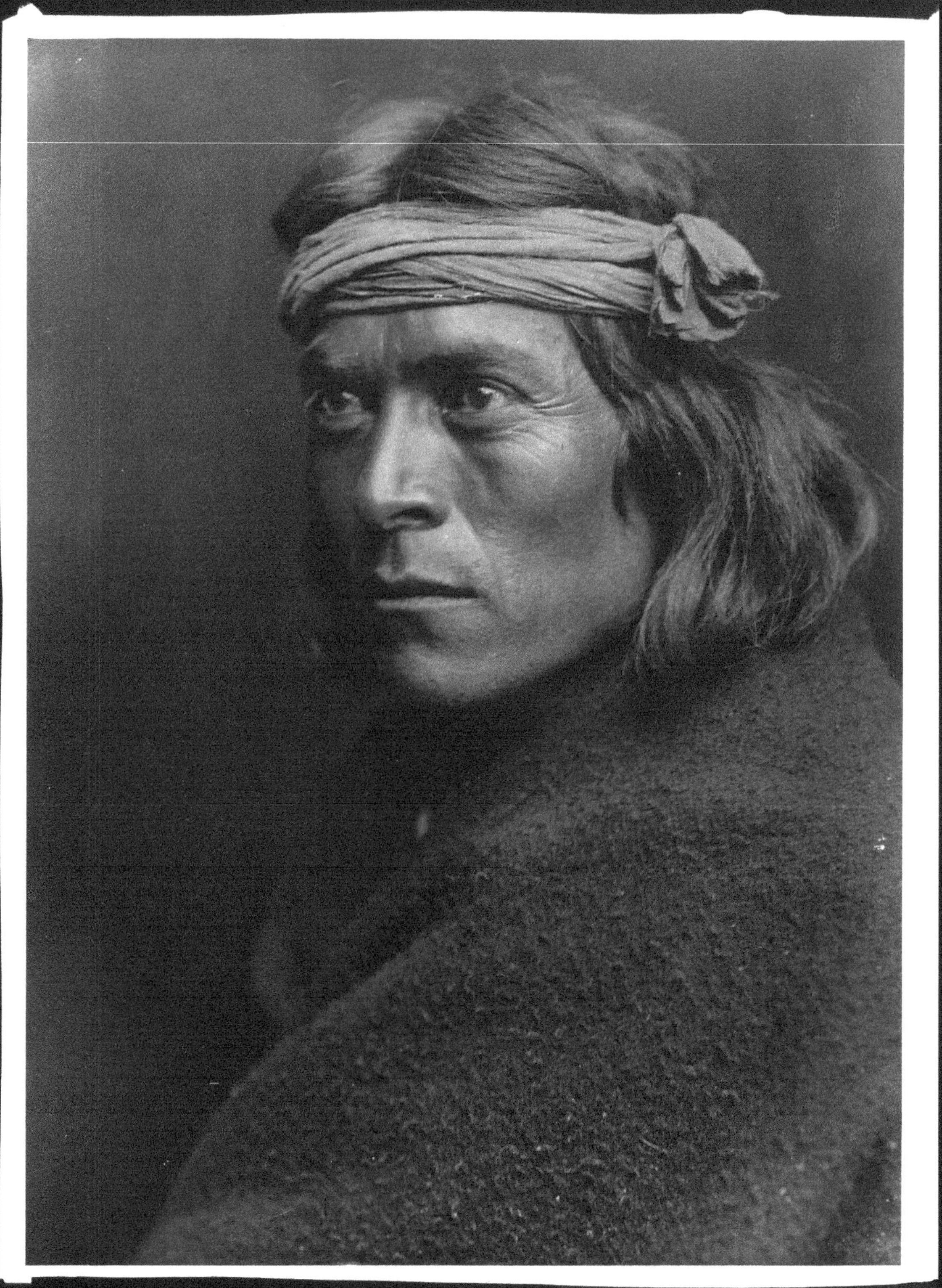

SKY-MOTHER AND SKY-FATHER (ZUNI)

The following narrative was recorded by Frank Cushing, an ethnologist who lived among the Zuni people of what is now western New Mexico from 1879 to 1881. As with the Seneca creation myth, the transcription was presented in the *Report of the Bureau of American Ethnology* (no. 32, 1891–92). Again, I have presented the text faithful to the original speaker, but with some minor editorial adaptations to remove possible confusions relating to archaic language:

'In the beginning, Awonawilona (the Maker and Container of All, the All-Father) alone had being. There was nothing else whatsoever throughout the great space of the ages except black darkness, and everywhere void desolation.

'In the beginning of creation, Awonawilona brought forth mists of increase, steams potent with growth, which evolved and uplifted. Thus, by means of his innate knowledge, the All-Container made himself in person and form of the Sun, whom we hold to be our father and who thus came to exist and appear. With his appearance came the brightening of the spaces with light, and with the brightening of the spaces the great mist-clouds were thickened together and fell, whereby was evolved water in water; yea, and the world-holding sea.

'With his substance of flesh outdrawn from the surface of his person, the Sun-Father formed the seed-stuff of twin worlds, impregnating them the great waters. And lo! In the heat of his light these waters of the sea grew green and mounds rose upon them, waxing wide and weighty until, behold! They became the "Four-fold Containing Mother-earth," and the "All-covering Father-sky."

'From the lying together of these two upon the great world waters, terrestrial life was conceived; whence began all beings of earth, men and the creatures, in the Four-fold womb of the World.

> WITH HIS SUBSTANCE OF FLESH OUTDRAWN FROM THE SURFACE OF HIS PERSON, THE SUN-FATHER FORMED THE SEED-STUFF OF TWIN WORLDS.

Left: A proud portrait of the Zuni governor Sat Sa, wearing a cloth headband and blanket, the photograph taken in the first decades of the 20th century by the American Edward Sheriff Curtis.

Right: Zuni petroglyphs depict the celebration of corn planting, the corn harvest and the Sun at the Village of the Great Kivas Anasazi ruins on the Zuni Indian Reservation in New Mexico.

'Thereupon the Earth-Mother repulsed the Sky-Father, growing big and sinking deep into the embrace of the waters below, thus separating from the Sky-Father in the embrace of the waters above. "How," said they to one another, "shall our children, when brought forth, know one place from another, even by the white light of the Sun-Father?"

'Now, like all the spirit beings the Earth-Mother and the Sky-Father were changeable, even as smoke in the wind; transmutable at thought, manifesting themselves in any form at will, like as dancers may by mask-making. Thus, as a man and woman they spoke to one another. "Behold!" said the Earth-Mother as a great terraced bowl appeared in her hand and within it water, "here the homes of my tiny children shall be. On the rim of each world-country they wander in, terraced mountains shall stand, making in one region many, whereby country shall be known from country, and within each, place from place. Behold, again!" said she as she spat on the water and rapidly stirred it with her fingers. Foam formed, gathering about the terraced rim, mounting higher and higher. "Yea," said she, "and from my bosom they shall draw nourishment, and they will find the substance of life as we were ourselves are sustained!" Then with her warm breath she blew across the terraces; white flecks of the foam broke away, and, floating

CREATION AND THE UNIVERSE

over above the water, were shattered by the cold breath of the Sky-Father attending, and showered downward an abundant fine mist and spray! "Even so, white clouds will float up from the great waters at the borders of the world and, clustering about the mountain terraces of the horizons, they be borne aloft and abroad by the breaths of the surpassing of soul-beings, and of the children, and shall hardened and broken be by your cold, raining down the water of life, even into the hollow places of my lap! For there will our children, mankind and creature-kind nestle, for warmth under your coldness."

> THEREUPON THE EARTH-MOTHER REPULSED THE SKY-FATHER, GROWING BIG AND SINKING DEEP INTO THE EMBRACE OF THE WATERS BELOW.

'Lo! Even the trees on high mountains near the clouds and the Sky-Father crouch low toward the Earth-Mother for warmth and protection! Warm is the Earth-Mother, cold the Sky-Father, even as woman is the warm, man the cold being! "Even so!" said the Sky-Father, "I will also be a help for our children, for behold!" And he spread his hand abroad with the palm downward and in all the wrinkles and crevices he brought forth shining yellow corn grains; in the dark of the early world-dawn they gleamed like sparks of fire, and moved

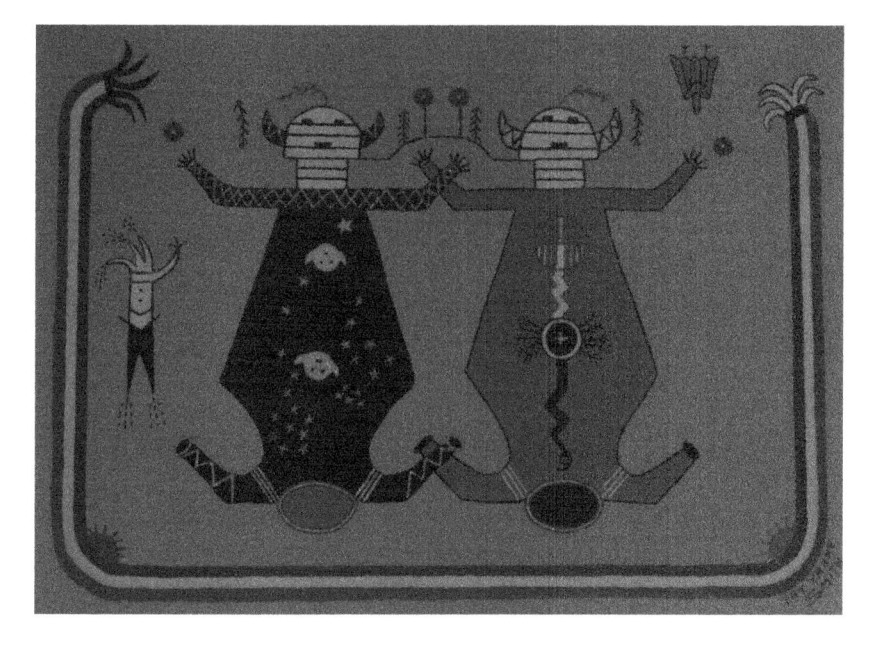

Left: This Navajo Indian sand painting shows the twin figures of Sky-Father (left) and Earth-Mother (right). The two beings maintain the balance of nature and the heavens.

as his hand was moved over the bowl, shining up from and also moving in the depths of the water therein. "See!" he said, pointing to the seven grains clasped by his thumb and four fingers, "by such shall our children be guided; for behold, when the Sun-Father is not nigh, and your terraces are in darkness, then shall our children be guided by lights – the lights of all the six regions turning round the centre… and even as these grains gleam up from the water, so shall numberless seed-grains spring up from your bosom when touched by my waters to nourish our children."

'Thus, and in other ways, they provided for their offspring. Then in the lowest of the four cave-wombs of the world, the seed of men and the creatures took form and increased; in the same way as eggs in warm places quickly produce worms, which growing, burst their shells and become birds, tadpoles or serpents, so did men and all creatures grow manifold and multiply in many kinds… everywhere were unfinished creatures, crawling like reptiles one over another in filth and black darkness, crowding thickly together and treading on each other, one spitting on another or doing indecent acts. Their murmurings and lamentations grew, until many among them sought to escape, growing wiser and more manlike.

'The Sun-Father thought carefully, and looking down he saw, on the great waters, a Foam-cap near to the Earth-Mother. With his sunbeam he impregnated and with his heat incubated the Foam-cap, and she gave birth to the Beloved Twins… first the Beloved Preceder, then the Beloved Follower, Twin brothers of Light, yet Elder and Younger, the Right and the Left, like a question and its answer. The Sun-Father gave to them his own knowledge and wisdom, in the same way that wise parents give their children understanding. He gave them himself and their mother the Foam-cap, the great cloud-bow and for arrows the thunderbolts of the four directions…

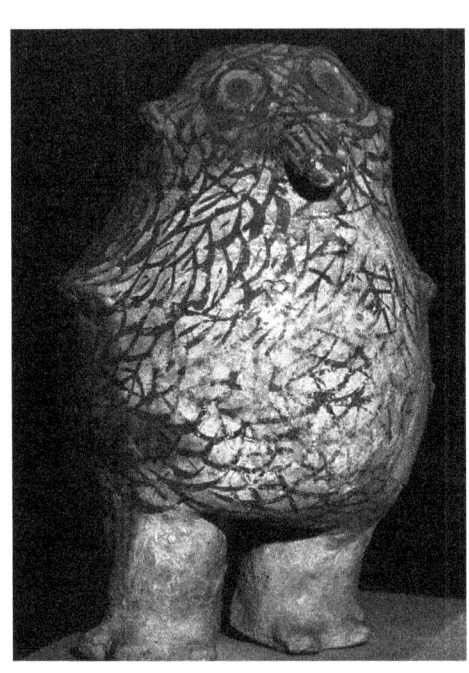

Above: A Zuni water vessel formed in the shape of an owl. The owl has traditionally been associated with death in Native American culture.

and the fog-making shield, which (spun of the floating clouds and spray, and woven, as of the cotton we spin and weave) floats on the wind, yet hides (as a shadow hides) its bearer, defending also. And to men and all creatures he gave them fathership and dominion, also as a man gives over the control of his work to the management of his hands. Having been instructed by the Sun-Father, they lifted the Sky-Father with their great cloud-bow into the heavens, so that the Earth became warm and thus more suited to their children, men and creatures. Then... they sped backwards swiftly on their floating fog-shield, westward to the Mountain of Generation. With their magic knives of the thunderbolt they opened up the mountain, and still on their cloud-shield – like a spider descending on her web – they went down into the dark of the underworld. There they lived with men and the creatures, attending them, coming to know them and becoming known of them as masters and fathers, seeking the ways of leading them.'

Above: A Bella Coola mask with a human face and an eagle's beak, representing a tribal ancestor that came to Earth as an eagle.

In every regard, this myth has a grandeur and scale to rival anything presented by Greek or Roman mythology. Creation is an act of divine muscle, the heavenly figures wrestling and sculpting the world with their formidable power. And yet there is also something deeply caring and recognizable about the god figures. The narrative has several points that emphasize the pastoral nature of the Sky-Mother and Sky-Father; they seek to provide for the people and creatures they create, not just send them out into a merciless world. Critically – and most visibly embodied in the Beloved Twins – they seek to bring forth balance and harmony, both of which are central concepts in Native American mythology. Implicit in such narratives, therefore, is a warning made explicit in many other myths – breaking the harmony of society, nature and tradition is disastrous, and punishment will surely follow. In a sense, Native American creation myths are as much cautionary as they are explanatory.

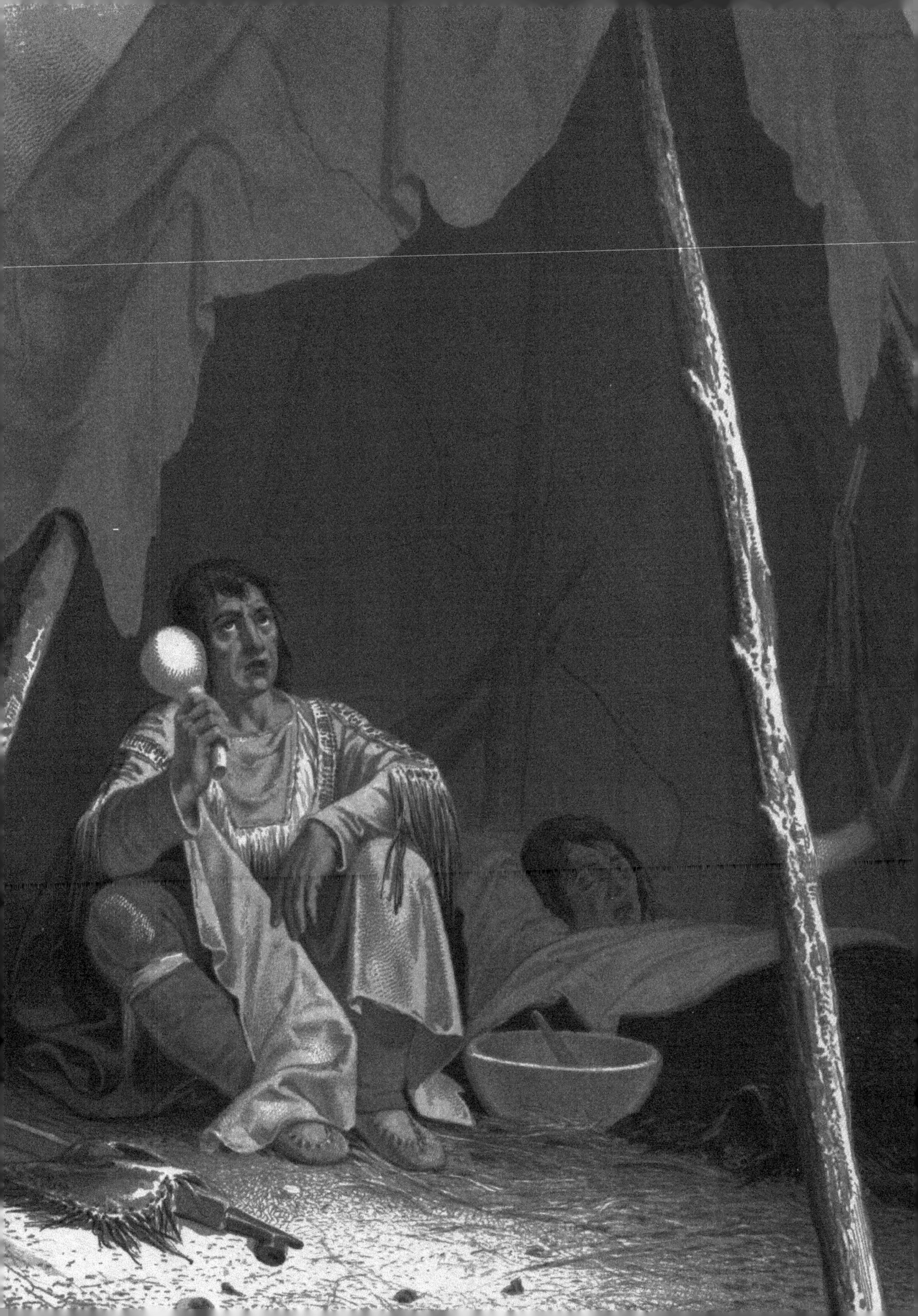

2

PEOPLE, FAMILY AND CULTURE

In traditional Native American culture, almost everything is imbued with meaning. Indeed, in this rich mythological landscape, every aspect of tribal culture – clothing, food, medicine, hunting, agriculture, housing, terrain, weather, pets, family, relationships and so on – at some point seems to have its own mythological narrative, one that describes either its genesis or its nature.

THE NATIVE American universe is holistic to its core, with all things existing together in various states of balance or imbalance, the latter usually caused by the actions of people taking no regard for their place within the natural order of things.

In this chapter, we look at a handful of the hundreds of myths and legends that explain either the origins of a particular people or a particular aspect of tribal culture. As with the narratives in the previous chapter, a huge variety of causes are involved – animals, weather, landscape, plants, meddling gods and spirits, all play their part in the rise of human culture. In

Left: A medicine man conducts a healing ceremony over a sick patient. The specific spells and rituals have been passed down over hundreds of years, each targeting a different spiritual or physical malady.

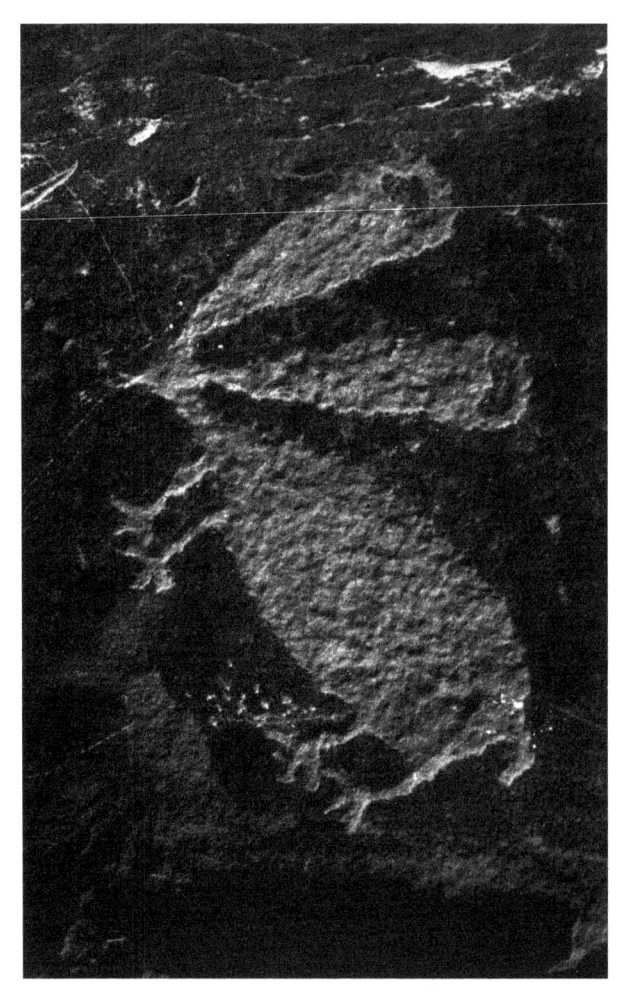

Above: A rabbit petroglyph in a rock in Wyoming. The rabbit features frequently in Native American mythology, associated with attributes such as fertility, survival, intelligence and even self-sacrifice.

essence, the whole world shares in the human project.

RABBIT BOY (WHITE RIVER SIOUX)

The White River Sioux were a tribe of the widespread Sioux people that, logically enough, lived along the mighty White River, a tributary of the Missouri River, running for nearly 966km (600 miles) through Nebraska and South Dakota. To modern eyes, the myth of the Rabbit Boy is a somewhat brutal tale that explains both the origin of a people while also reflecting on the nature of human jealousy and attraction. It is one of many myths that feature a rabbit as a quirky central character. This focus might appear puzzling, as the rabbit seems to be one of the lesser creatures of the natural world, certainly compared to majestic animals such as the eagle, bear and wolf. Yet from the Native American perspective, the rabbit was significant because of its commonality. Not only was it a trickster on account of its nimbleness and survivor's intelligence, but its role as prey to many carnivores (and to humans) meant that its life had a symbolic connotation of sacrifice for the common good.

We see this in the story of the Rabbit Boy. The myth begins in a time beyond history, when the world was still in flux and the lines between human and animal society were indivisible. In this time there lived a humble rabbit, friendly and playful, who one day discovered a round ball-like clot of blood lying on the ground. Instinctively he kicked it, and in applying motion to the blood clot he gave it the energy of life. As he rolled it along the ground, each kick made the blood clot expand and take shape, and eventually it took the form of a human – Rabbit Boy.

PEOPLE, FAMILY AND CULTURE 45

Now rabbit and his wife had no children, so they took Rabbit Boy as their own, loving him, raising him and dressing him in the finest clothes. Slowly the Rabbit Boy grew from infant to adolescent without any meaningful recognition of the biological differences between him and his parents. Eventually the rabbit, now ageing, took him to one side and explained that despite their love for him, he was actually a human being and would have to leave the world of animals to live among people.

So Rabbit Boy set out on a quest to find others like himself. He eventually came to a village where the reception to his arrival was mixed. The people wondered where he was from, as at that time there was no other village in existence. In addition, Rabbit Boy was dressed in a stunning and highly decorative buckskin coat that made some of the boys in the village jealous. This situation was made worse by the fact that Rabbit Boy quickly fell in love with the most beautiful girl among them, who also fell in love with him because of his looks and his clothes, but also because of his aura of wisdom and his kind spirit.

Below: Hopi warriors hunting rabbits. The speed and dexterity of the rabbit earned it a reputation as a trickster, using its wits to outsmart its prey.

The ringleader of those villagers against Rabbit Boy was the trickster Spider Man – Iktome – who had some skill in the arts of sorcery and magic, and was also deeply in love with the beautiful girl. Colluding with other boys, Iktome first sneaked up on Rabbit Boy and threw a magical hoop over him, which apparently rendered him unable to move. In fact, Rabbit Boy was only pretending to be imprisoned – his own magical power was far greater than that of Iktome. The village boys then tied Rabbit Boy to a tree, and Iktome persuaded them to kill him with knives and cut up his body. Seeing his demise approaching, Rabbit Boy chanted a death song:

> *Friends, friends,*
> *I have fought the sun.*
> *He tried to burn me up,*
> *But he could not do it.*
> *Even battling the sun,*
> *I held my own.*

The listeners could not know it, but Rabbit Boy had long had a vision of wrestling with the sun, yet always winning in the ostensibly unequal battle between rabbit and star. Following his chant, our protagonist was murdered and his body chopped up into little pieces and dropped into a soup.

Little did his killers know that their actions had simply made Rabbit Boy stronger. He ascended into heaven, riding a beam of sunlight, where his body – this time of even greater strength and wisdom – was remade inside the sun. The villagers' medicine man had seen his ascent and warned that Rabbit Boy would soon return, at which point they should let him marry the beautiful girl. Iktome, bristling with indignation, decided that the villagers should also tie him up and dismember him, so that his power could then rival that of the Rabbit Boy. Before he was killed, he attempted to repeat the Rabbit Boy's chant, but the recantation was fatally inaccurate:

> LITTLE DID HIS KILLERS KNOW THAT THEIR ACTIONS HAD SIMPLY MADE RABBIT BOY STRONGER.

*Friends, friends,
I have fought the moon.
She tried to fight,
But I won.
Even battling the moon,
I came out on top.*

Because of his failure to remember the words correctly, Iktome did not rise again after his death, whereas the Rabbit Boy returned to take his place at the heart of the village, building a new generation of Sioux with his beautiful wife.

In many ways, the story of the Rabbit Boy is largely a morality tale, warning the listener against the evils of jealousy and arrogance. But given its temporal setting in the very earliest days of the Sioux community, it is also establishing a kind of spiritual genetics – the Rabbit Boy's wisdom, integrity and strength overriding death itself, and passing these attributes on to future generations of Sioux Indians, rather than the malice of Iktome.

Above: A Sioux encampment on the Upper Missouri River. The tipis were perfect homes for life on the Great Plains, being simple to erect and protective against both wind and rain.

THE BLACKFOOT GENESIS AND THE ORIGINS OF MARRIAGE (BLACKFOOT)

Many of the Native American myths about tribal origins work on the basis of people already being in existence. Some other myths, however, look at the origin of tribes as an act of creation through the wisdom of a guiding individual. A key character in this context is 'Old Man', a figure who recurs frequently in several strands of Blackfoot mythology. In essence, the Old Man is equivalent to the 'Great Spirit', a power of both creative force and also eternal wisdom, reflected in the general veneration given to elderly individuals in Native American society.

In the Blackfoot genesis story, the Old Man wandered the Earth in the earliest days of creation, forming the plants,

THE SEVEN FIRES PROPHECY

IN NATIVE AMERICAN CULTURE, there are often mythologies that transcend several tribes, uniting them in a shared vision of their people and their destiny. One such example is the 'Seven Fires Prophecy' of the Anishinaabe, the word referring to a broad grouping of culturally related tribes in the northeast of the United States and the western parts of Canada. (Specific people falling under this category include the Algonquin, Chippewa, Odawa, Oji-Cree, Ojibwe, Potawatomi and Mississaugas.) The Seven Fires Prophecy is essentially a vision of the unfolding of time in seven different epochs or 'fires', the vision for each given by a different prophet. The prophecies also signify a sense of both spiritual and physical migration, each stage of the journey defined by decisions and discoveries. In summary, the content of the prophecies is as follows:

First fire – The Anishinaabe nation rises, gathering around the Sacred Shell of the Midewiwin Lodge. To avoid certain destruction, they set out on a journey, with seven stops along the way, to find their chosen ground – a turtle-shaped island of great fertility.

Second fire – While camped by water, this will be a period of decline for the people, a move away from their spiritual life. However, a boy born among them will show the way back to traditional life and values.

Third fire – This prophecy brought another stage in the migration, as the reinvigorated people find the path to the chosen land once again. They will recognize the chosen land because food grows upon water there.

Fourth fire – This prophecy was delivered by two prophets, each bearing a very different message about the coming of the 'light-skinned race' – the white people. The prophets told the Anishinaabe that the white people would come with one of two 'faces' – the face of brotherhood or the face of death. The Anishinaabe were to judge what face they brought and to act accordingly.

Fifth fire – The fifth fire is a time of great struggle, in which the Anishinaabe people are tempted by new ways of living, abandoning the old traditions in the process. The prophecy comes as a warning, admonishing the people that if they reject the old ways they will bring destruction upon themselves.

Sixth fire – The fifth-fire prophecy comes to fruition in the sixth fire, as the age-old culture begins to collapse under the influence of false promises and new ways of living. Societal bonds break down, resulting in disloyalty and individualism, and life becomes out of balance with nature and family.

Seventh fire – The seventh fire brings restoration, as the Anishinaabe once more find the trail to the promised land and a fresh generation rediscovers their roots, resulting in a period of rebirth. The new people are cautioned to remain strong in their quest, otherwise the restoration will be threatened.

Opposite: An evocative photograph of a Chippewa camp. The Chippewa have been concentrated deep in the woodlands in the northeastern United States and eastern Canada.

animals and landscape with the power of his own will. One day he fashioned a woman and her child – a son – out of clay, declaring that 'You must be people', i.e. the Blackfoot. He also established the laws of life and death, noting that – following the death of the woman's young son – 'People will have to die.'

But having created the Blackfoot, he also needed to nurture their survival and society. Here the story is continued by George Bird Grinnell, another US anthropologist of the 19th century who did posterity a considerable service by collecting the oral traditions of the Blackfoot, which he recounted in his *Blackfoot Lodge Tales* (1892). Here the narrator explains how Old Man looked after the early Blackfoot people, not only promoting their physical existence but also bringing forth a spiritual dimension:

Above: George Bird Grinnell, the naturalist, explorer and anthropologist who collected dozens of Native American myths during the late 1800s and early 1900s.

Right: The *Blackfoot Lodge Tales* by George Bird Grinnell, who recorded myths primarily from the Blackfoot, Cheyenne and Pawnee.

'The first people were poor and naked, and did not know how to get a living. Old Man showed them the roots and berries, and told them that they could eat them; that in a certain month of the year they could peel the bark off some trees and eat it, that it was good. He told the people that the animals should be their food, and gave them to the people, saying, "These are your herds." He said: "All these little animals that live in the ground – rats, squirrels, skunks, beavers – are good to eat. You need not fear to eat of their flesh." He made all the birds that fly, and told the people that there was no harm in their flesh, that it could be eaten. The first people that he created he used to take about through the timber and swamps and over the prairies, and show them the different plants. Of a certain plant he would say, "The root of this plant, if gathered in a certain month of the year, is good for a certain sickness." So they learned the power of all herbs.

'In those days there were buffalo. Now the people had no arms, but those black animals with long beards were armed; and once, as the people were moving about, the buffalo saw them, and ran after them, and hooked them, and killed and ate them. One day, as the Maker of the people was travelling over the country, he saw some of his children that he had made, lying dead, torn to pieces and partly eaten by the buffalo. When he saw this he was very sad. He said: "This will not do. I will change this. The people shall eat the buffalo."

'He went to some of the people who were left, and said to them, "How is it that you people do nothing to these animals that are killing you?" The people said: "What can we do? We have no way to kill these animals, while they are armed and can kill us." Then said the Maker: "That is not hard. I will make you a weapon that will kill these animals." So he went out, and cut some sarvis berry shoots, and brought them in, and peeled the bark off them. He took a larger piece of wood, and flattened it, and tied a string to it, and made a bow. Now, as he was the master of all birds and could do with them as he wished, he went out and caught one, and took feathers from its wing, and split them, and tied them to the shaft of wood. He tied four feathers along the shaft, and tried the arrow at a mark, and found that it did not fly well. He took these feathers off, and put on three; and when he tried it again, he found that it was good. He went out and began to break sharp pieces off the stones. He tried them, and found that the black flint stones made the best arrow points, and some white flints. Then he taught the people how to use these things.

Below: A Blackfoot hunter with his bow and arrow – multiple arrows held at the ready – watches the terrain intently for any sign of movement.

Below: A famous depiction of a Native American buffalo hunt. Many of the tribes in the North American interior and plains were utterly dependent on the buffalo for their way of life.

'Then he said: "The next time you go out, take these things with you, and use them as I tell you, and do not run from these animals. When they run at you, as soon as they get pretty close, shoot the arrows at them, as I have taught you; and you will see that they will run from you or will run in a circle around you."

'Now, as people became plenty, one day three men went out on to the plain to see the buffalo, but they had no arms. They saw the animals, but when the buffalo saw the men, they ran after them and killed two of them, but one got away. One day after this, the people went on a little hill to look about, and the buffalo saw them, and said, "*Saiyah*, there is some more of our food," and they rushed on them. This time the people did not run. They began to shoot at the buffalo with the bows and arrows *Na'pi* had given them, and the buffalo began to fall; but in the fight a person was killed.

'At this time these people had flint knives given them, and they cut up the bodies of the dead buffalo. It is not healthful to eat the meat raw, so Old Man gathered soft dry rotten driftwood and made punk of it, and then got a piece of hard wood, and drilled a hole in it with an arrow point, and gave them a pointed piece of hard wood, and taught them how to make a fire with fire sticks, and to cook the flesh of these animals and eat it.

'They got a kind of stone that was in the land, and then took another harder stone and worked one upon the other, and hollowed out the softer one, and made a kettle of it. This was the fashion of their dishes.

'Also Old Man said to the people: "Now, if you are overcome, you may go and sleep, and get power. Something will come to you in your dream that will help you. Whatever these animals tell you to do, you must obey them, as they appear to you in your sleep. Be guided by them. If anybody wants help, if you are alone and travelling, and cry aloud for help, your prayer will be answered. It may be by the eagles, perhaps by the buffalo, or by the bears. Whatever animal answers your prayer, you must listen to him." That was how the first people got through the world, by the power of their dreams.'

Above: A Blackfoot medicine man, his human form obscured by his ceremonial outfit. The medicine man could mediate between the physical world and the spirit world.

This narrative is extraordinary for the fusion of deep spirituality with intense practicality. Old Man literally guides the early Blackfoot through the step-by-step production of bows and arrows, flint knives, firesticks and cooking vessels. On top of that, he also gives the people dreams as an ethereal meeting place for spiritual guides, a place for acquiring wisdom and offering up prayers.

So it was that in Blackfoot society, even the humblest of objects and the most common of psychological events would have a mythological foundation. But the utility of the Old Man did not end there. In another myth, particularly shared among the Piegan Blackfeet of the North American Great Plains, the Old Man also plays an intermediary role in the familial building block of Native American society, the union of man and woman.

In the act of creation, Old Man brought forth human beings but separated men and women, who lived in different parts of the world. The cultures of men and women were initially similar, both spending much of their time hunting buffalo by herding them over cliffs. Over time some distinctions crept in. Men became more refined at hunting, having acquired bows and arrows, while women were talented in making fine clothes and attractive tipis. This got Old Man thinking. He suddenly realized that not only should men and women live together, but also that they should make love to one another as a pleasurable experience to unite the two genders and support the reproduction of future generations.

> IN THE ACT OF CREATION, OLD MAN BROUGHT FORTH HUMAN BEINGS BUT SEPARATED MEN AND WOMEN, WHO LIVED IN DIFFERENT PARTS OF THE WORLD.

So Old Man set out to conduct a reconnaissance of the female village to see how they lived. After four days and four nights of travel, he found a position behind some trees from which to observe the women's camp. What he saw – an ordered society with excellent handicraft skills (particularly in the working of buffalo hide) and physical grace – impressed him greatly, and he hurried back to the male camp to tell of what he had seen. As it happened, however, the chief of the women's village discovered Old Man's tracks and sent one of the young women of the village to follow them to their source. So the young woman also made the four-day journey and watched the men in life and work. She was also impressed, but more so by the physical strength of the menfolk and their more efficient skills in hunting that brought them a more bounteous and diverse larder. She went back to her village to tell the women of what she had seen, just as Old Man had recounted his observations to the men.

Now began something of a comedy of errors. The men decided to go to see the women for themselves, but when they turned up looking bedraggled, messy and covered in dirt, the women were horrified and screamed at them to go away. The men retreated, with even Old Man saying 'Women are dangerous. I shouldn't have created them.' But then both sides reconsidered. The men decided to try to impress the women by washing, cleaning their hair and dressing in the finest clothes they could make. Even Old Man took a sweat bath and a swim in a lake to improve his acceptability. At the same time, however, the chief in the women's village decided to meet the men in their buffalo-butchering clothes, hoping that their unkempt appearance would make the

Above: Blackfeet women on horseback are here moving camp; they are dragging the long tipi tripod poles behind them, using these poles as a simple travois to carry other goods.

men feel at ease. Instead, when the two parties met again, the men were appalled at how rough and ready the blood-encrusted women looked and retreated in disgust.

So the woman chief had a rethink and decided to have one last go at making a connection with the men. She told all the women to make themselves as beautiful as they possibly could. After bathing, they braided and decorated their hair, put on

Left: Blackfoot men and women raise their voices in song outside a tipi. They hold a variety of objects, including coup sticks and a modern firearm.

beautiful doeskin robes, wore ornate jewellery made from bones, shells and quills, and reddened their cheeks with make-up. Thus adorned, they set out again for the men's village. Old Man heard of their approach in advance, and while some of the men recommended preparing for war, Old Man calmed the mood and instead told everyone to dress in their finery, their clothes decorated with feathers, fur and bear claws.

Finally the men and women met, with everyone looking their best. It was a moment of revelation, and sparks of attraction and desire flew between them, and between Old Man and the woman chief, who made love with one another. Such was their enthusiasm for this newfound experience that they went to tell all the others – but they needn't have bothered, as when they got back to the now-empty camp they found that the men and women had been perfectly capable of discovering sex all on their own. Thus it was that a physical and mental happiness entered the world, love was discovered and children came forth. The women moved into the men's camp to live there, becoming wives in the process, but also bringing with them all the skills they had to improve village life for the men. In turn, the men went out to hunt for the women, providing for their physical needs. Thus Blackfoot family and society was born.

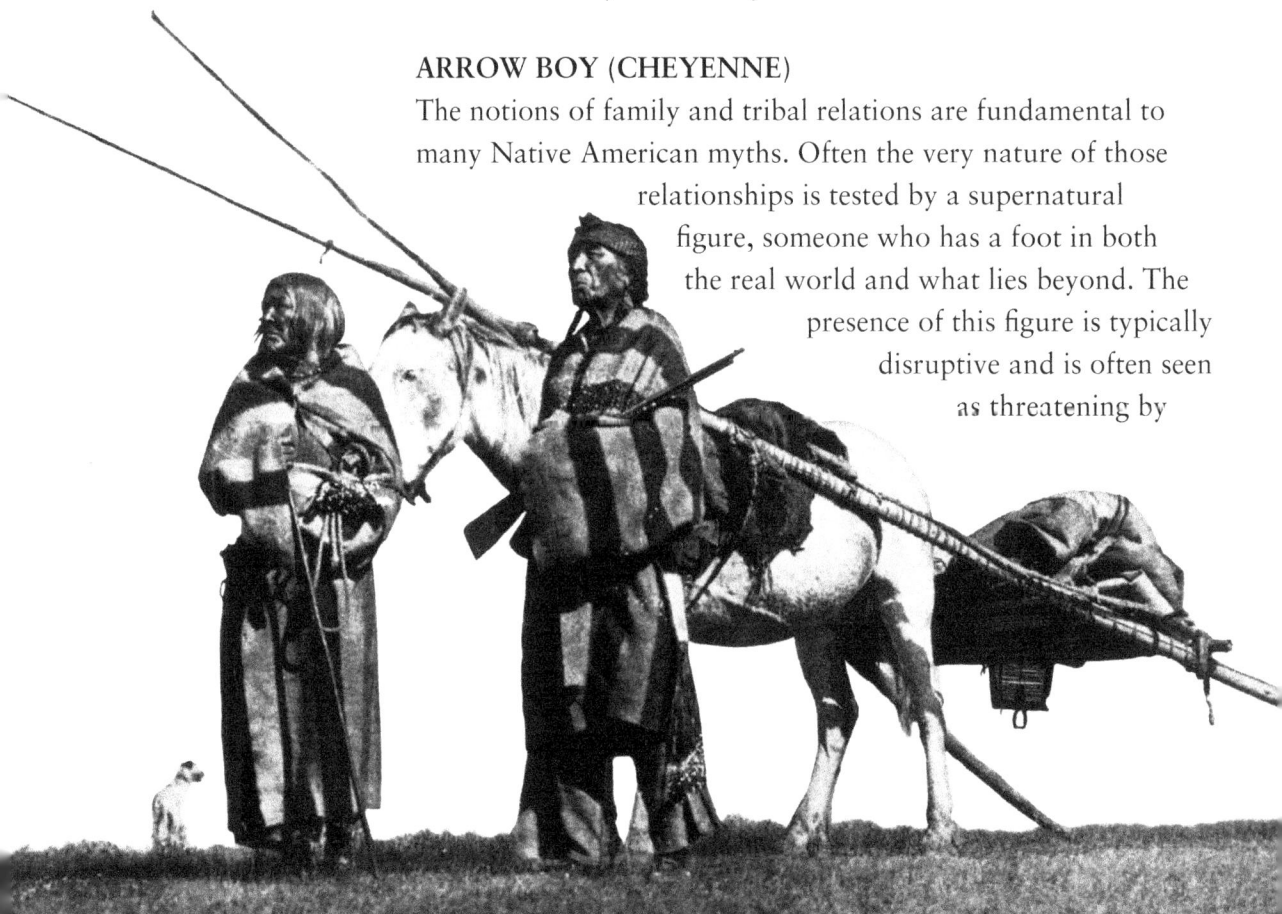

ARROW BOY (CHEYENNE)

The notions of family and tribal relations are fundamental to many Native American myths. Often the very nature of those relationships is tested by a supernatural figure, someone who has a foot in both the real world and what lies beyond. The presence of this figure is typically disruptive and is often seen as threatening by

Below: A Blackfoot man and woman on their travels. They are wearing trade blankets sold to them by the European colonists.

other members of the tribe. Yet by the end of the narrative, the exceptional being has established a new tradition or set of values within the people, thereby improving tribal integrity and health.

A classic example of this type of myth is that of the Arrow Boy told by the Cheyenne, but with variant stories among other nations such as the Sioux and Pueblos. The story begins with a pregnancy, a natural event that augured extraordinary events when the young woman's pregnancy extended to four years. Finally, at the end of this exceptional gestation, she gave birth to a beautiful baby boy. As so often happens in Native American myths, however, the parents died and so the boy went to live a lonely life with his grandmother.

From the earliest of years, it was clear that there was something unusual about the boy. He acquired all the basic skills of human development with unusual speed, progressing from walking and talking through to hunting with preternatural ability. Most noticeably, he also demonstrated a fascination and affinity for the practices of the tribal medicine men.

It is important not confuse the concept of the 'medicine man' with that of a modern alternative medicine practitioner. Instead, the Native American medicine man was a spiritual healer, using chants, talismans, ceremonies and rituals to cure someone of spiritual maladies, albeit maladies often expressed as physical illnesses.

When he reached the age of 10, the boy sought and was granted an audience with the medicine men of his tribe. He sat in their midst in their lodge, where they performed various rituals and magical feats. Then the boy, emboldened with his supernatural powers, made an extraordinary demonstration. Having first painted his body in red and black paint, he wafted a

Above: A Cheyenne medicine man (centre), holding a medicine stick used in the performance of rituals.

60 PEOPLE, FAMILY AND CULTURE

strong bowstring through the ceremonial incense, then wrapped it around his neck and covered himself with a robe. He told the other men in the room to grip the loose ends of the bowstring and then pull on them with all their strength. They did so, horrified when the boy's decapitated head suddenly rolled out from beneath the robe. They put the head back, and when they lifted the robe up an old man was sitting beneath it. Three more times they replaced and lifted the robe, and each time revealed a different state beneath – first a pile of human bones, next nothing at all and finally the boy returned in perfect health.

He was lauded as a powerful addition to the circle of medicine men, but that status was about to change. During an altercation between the boy and the chief of the tribe, Young Wolf, over the butchering of a buffalo carcass – the chief repeatedly pushed the boy off the carcass, saying he wanted the hide for a robe, even though the boy had killed the animal – the boy struck and killed the chief with a buffalo leg. Infuriated, the tribe's warriors decided that the boy must be killed. They tracked him down to his grandmother's lodge, but when he saw them he kicked over a cooking pot onto the fire and magically disappeared in the smoke. The warriors ran outside, only to see the boy in the distance walking off to the east. They chased him, but no matter how fast they went they never seemed to get any closer.

Eventually, the boy appeared to his pursuers on top of a nearby hill. On five separate occasions he appeared, each time wearing a different form of elaborate warrior dress, his body painted in bright colours. After his fifth appearance, however, he disappeared from view, and it was at this time that a dreadful famine descended upon the Cheyenne people. Hunger and starvation stalked through the Cheyenne villages, the people looking in vain to their spells and rituals to break the cycle.

The boy, meanwhile, was continuing onwards with his physical and spiritual journey. He ascended a high mountain and passed through a mystical entrance into the interior of the

> WHEN HE SAW THEM HE KICKED OVER A COOKING POT ONTO THE FIRE AND MAGICALLY DISAPPEARED IN THE SMOKE.

Far left: An early photograph – another studio shot from Edward Sheriff Curtis – of Hastobiga, a Navaho medicine man.

Above: A Cheyenne altar set inside a tent, with a buffalo skull surrounded by boughs and sticks with feathers; additional sticks and feathers are lined up on both sides, forming a ritual pattern on the ground.

Earth. Inside, he encountered a group of wise old men who offered him a seat in their circle. They also presented him with a medicine bundle – specific to the Cheyenne – wrapped in fox fur and containing a number of sacred arrows. From this point forth the boy would be known as Arrow Boy. The elders instructed him in the use of the bundle for four years, during which time he became a medicine man of great power, able to perform magic that would influence all aspects of tribal life.

Once the four years had passed, Arrow Boy left the mountain and returned to his people. Famine still cast a long shadow over the Cheyenne – the buffalo on which they depended had been terribly absent from the plains around them. But now Arrow Boy brought his newfound power to the people. Having performed a demonstration of his magic by turning some dry buffalo bones into fresh meat, he then gathered the villagers and taught them sacred incantations using the arrows in his medicine bundle. When it came to the song of the fourth arrow, the air filled with dust and there was a rumble like thunder – the buffalo had returned. That night, the Cheyenne people slept in peace and awoke the next day to undertake a great hunt, their larders filled to overflowing with buffalo meat and hides.

Arrow Boy is a legendary figure in the history of the Cheyenne people and is also known as the prophet Motseyoef, who has appeared at various points in the tribal chronology, each

MEDICINE BUNDLE

THE MEDICINE BUNDLE WAS, and remains, a holy object within a Native American tribe. It is typically a leather, hide, wool or fabric wrap or bag, with most examples measuring 30.5–35.5cm (12–14in), although examples of bundles held by an entire tribe (rather than by specific individuals) can be larger with more substantial contents. Inside the bag are various objects, often humble in themselves but each representing a different spiritual significance. Items might include animal teeth, rocks, crystals, arrowheads, tobacco, plant specimens, human hair, beads or bones. The contents are subject to change over time, with objects being added according to the spiritual events of the tribe as the medicine bundle is passed down to others over the generations. The objects within the bundle are utilized in spells and rituals, and the package is usually opened only at certain sacred times or events. If used properly and accompanied by the right sacrifices and practices, the medicine bundle can bring great benefits to both the tribe and to individuals, including better fortune in hunting, improvements in health, victory in war and beneficial changes in the weather. Given the status of the medicine bundle, it is little wonder that it is treated with such reverence, with only certain people able to handle it, and the objects inside are never placed on the bare ground.

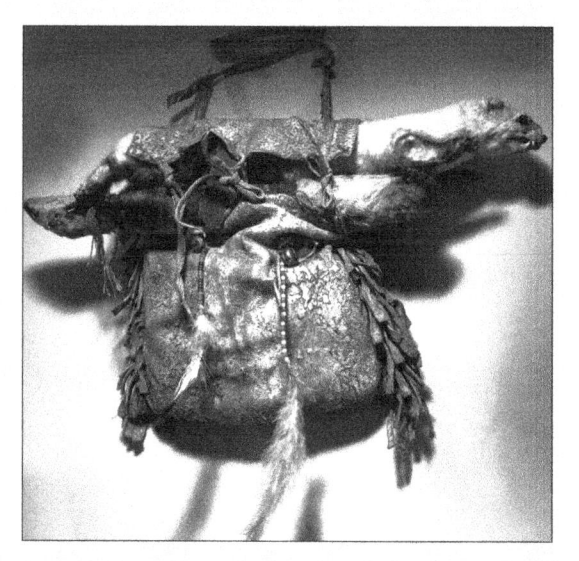

Above: The power of the sacred bundle emanates from each object individually, but also from the collective power of the bundle.

Left: Medicine bundles are sacred artefacts, treated with the same reverence that Christian traditions hold for relics of the saints or the cross.

time his appearance bringing either a warning or a blessing. It was Motseyoef, for example, who warned his people of the coming of the white man to North America, with all the tragic consequences that entailed. Yet the story of the Arrow Boy is one that anchors a community around a physical artefact: the medicine arrows. These are preserved and revered to this day by the Cheyenne Arrow Keeper, which is a sacred duty. Arrow Boy's medicine bundle is not merely a historical object, but rather a physical link to the presence of Arrow Boy/Motseyoef; an object that is the embodiment of a founding community myth.

Below: A simple fibre storage bag, used to gather plants, foods and medicine by Native American people in California.

THE ORIGINS OF NATURAL MEDICINE (CHEROKEE)

In Native American culture we can distinguish between two types of medicine, although this involves imposing a rather Western non-holistic viewpoint. On the one hand there is spiritual medicine, designed to help individuals or the tribe to tackle psychological maladies or practical problems with spiritual causes. On the other, there was the practice of treating physical ailments with herbs or medicinal plants. In reality, the two categories are rather artificial, as in Native American culture there is not the cut-and-dry division between physical and spiritual that we tend to impose in modern life. Indeed, many of the plants used in the remedies had their own accompanying mythology and were frequently treated as sacred materials with their own special place in tribal history and culture.

Cherokee lore includes an explanation of how medicine itself was created for the benefit of humankind. The story begins in halcyon days, when animals and humans lived together side by side without violence or predation, even conversing with one another in a shared language. But over time, the human population expanded and there became competition for resources and food. Furthermore, human beings eventually turned to hunting animals for their meat and skins. As a result, the balance of nature was broken.

The elders of the bear tribe decided to resist the encroachment of people and gathered together in council around their chief, White Bear. Together they discussed various strategies for countering the humans. The first idea was that the bears themselves should produce bows and arrows, and learn to use them in warfare. It soon became apparent that this idea was a non-starter, as a bear's claws prevented him from operating the bowstring properly, and cutting his claws to do so would result in his starvation as he would no longer be able to climb trees to find food.

Meanwhile the deer tribe council, also locked in conversation about what to do regarding the humans, arrived at a more sophisticated solution. Through magic, they imposed a terrible rheumatic illness upon any hunter who killed a deer without the proper reverence or ritual. Chief Little Deer sent a messenger to the chief of the Cherokee tribe, telling him that before killing a deer the hunter should first offer prayer, asking the deer for pardon and explaining that he is only hunting to prevent his people from starving. If this ritual was not performed, Chief Little Deer would find out by consulting the dead deer's spirit, at which point the hunter would become crippled and no longer able to hunt or otherwise provide for his tribe.

The fish and the reptiles also held council. They chose to place a spiritual curse upon the Cherokee. Their vengeance

Below: This image shows a Zuni man grinding medicine and natural pigments. Nature provided its own pharmacy to the Native American tribes.

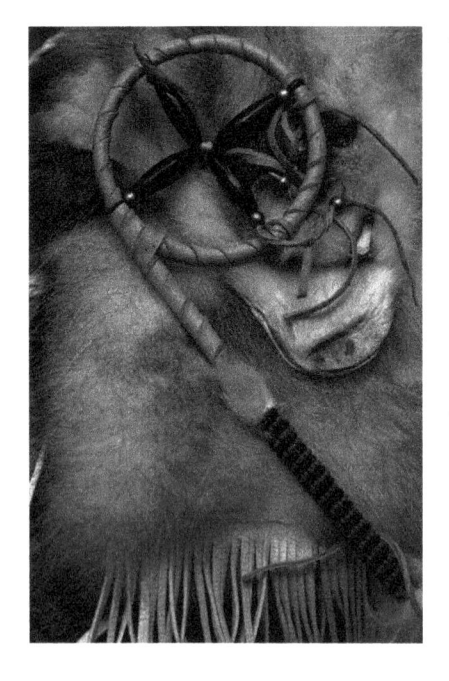

was to visit sleeping hunters in their dreams, terrifying them with nightmares of monstrous snakes and garish fish. The Cherokee shamans were therefore locked in a dream-world battle to defend their people from these disturbing visions.

One by one, the different classes of animals imposed physical or spiritual penalties upon the Cherokee for hunting them. But now the plants – who regarded human beings in a more favourable light – got involved. They decided to protect humans with their medicinal properties, with every tree, shrub, herb, grass and moss contributing a cure for the ailments inflicted by the animals. They also held consultations with the Cherokee shaman, finding cures for the more difficult conditions. So it was the Cherokee gained medicine.

Above: A Cherokee medicine bag with a 'healing wheel' or 'sacred hoop', which symbolized the four dimensions of the world and the repeated cycle of life itself.

THE BEAR FAMILY (PENOBSCOT)

In Native American myths and legends, 'family' is an extensive concept that includes the traditional nuclear family but goes well beyond it into the sense of tribal family, and possibly even further into considerations of the animal kingdom and the natural world being part of a community's spiritual belonging. What is important is that the individual considers himself or herself part of the greater whole, and demonstrates commitment to that family.

A powerful myth of familial loyalty comes from the Penobscot Nation, traditionally settled in what is today Maine, the most northeastern point in the US. This is the legend of the bear family. So the story goes, a Penobscot man, his wife and their young son set out on a journey to Canada, heading to attend a council and dance to be held at the Iroquois village of Caughnawaga. At one point in the journey, the man paddled upriver in a canoe while his wife stayed behind with the boy to pack up. The boy, however, ran ahead without his mother's knowledge, intending to catch up with his father, but became lost in the process. When his parents discovered this they were distraught, and all the men of the village turned out to look for him, but to no avail.

Far right: Members of the Arikara tribe of North Dakota perform a medicine ceremony; music and chant were often integral to such rituals.

Many months later, human and bear footprints were found together on the banks of a nearby river alongside sharpened sticks used for hunting fish. The villagers concluded that the boy was still alive, but had been adopted by a bear family. Another search party was sent out, this time including a particularly lazy man from the village who only joined the hunt after being shamed into doing so. The lazy man eventually found the bear den. Inside, as the villagers had guessed, was the boy who had been cared for by the bears – father-bear, mother-bear and baby-bear. The lazy man knocked on the rocks outside the den and the bears inside were troubled.

> INSIDE, AS THE VILLAGERS HAD GUESSED, WAS THE BOY WHO HAD BEEN CARED FOR BY THE BEARS – FATHER-BEAR, MOTHER-BEAR AND BABY-BEAR.

Father-bear decided to venture out with a placatory gift for the lazy man – a birch-bark drinking vessel – but when he went to the entrance the lazy man shot him dead with his bow and arrow. The mother-bear then went to the entrance, where she was also shot and killed. The baby-bear also went and suffered the same fate.

Now the lazy man entered the den, finding the boy crouching terrified in a corner, distraught at the loss of his bear family. The lazy man picked him up and carried him back to the village, where the boy was returned to his jubilant parents and the lazy man became rich through gifts of gratitude from all the villagers. Yet the boy was not grateful, and terribly missed the bears who had been his protectors and his family. In physical response the boy began turning into a bear himself, with fur growing out of his body and his voice becoming deep and gruff. However, the

Below: A portrait of members of the Penobscot Nation, who are believed to have inhabited territory around Maine for some 11,000 years.

love of his parents eventually counteracted the transformation and he returned to being human once more. As an adult, he married and had his own children, creating a new family. Yet he, and all his descendants, declared themselves to be bears, stating proudly that 'I am one of the Bear family.'

The moral of this myth works on many different levels and, as is common in such tales, contains some ambiguity. Was the lazy man wrong to take the boy away from his bear family and return him to his parents? Killing the bears certainly seems an act of judgement, and in many ways the bears appear nobler than the humans. But the boy and his descendants recognize this nobility and also link their family identity to that of the bears. Ultimately, the message seems to be that family is an inclusive concept, something as much defined by acts of kindness and caring as it is by genetic origins.

Above: A Navajo shaman giving medicine. In traditional Native American medicine, illness is often regarded as a problem with part-spiritual origins.

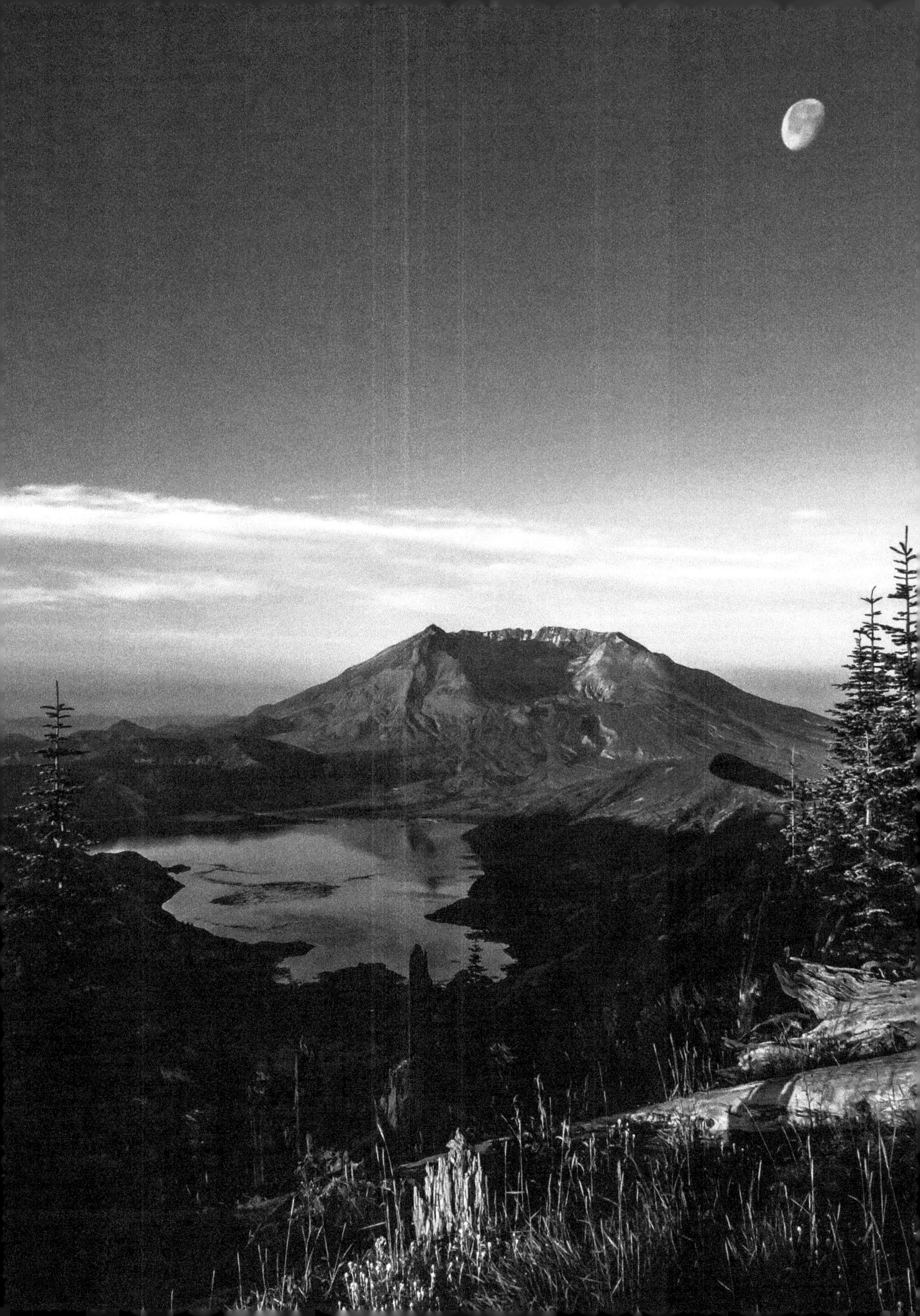

3
THE NATURAL WORLD

We have already seen how intrinsic the natural world is to Native American myths and legends. Indeed, it is actually hard to find many of their narratives that don't intersect strongly with natural elements, be they plants, animals or features of the landscape.

THIS IS entirely understandable in subsistence agriculture or hunter-gatherer communities, whose entire existence was intertwined with seasonal conditions, the migration or accessibility of animals, the growth and death of plants, and the contours and limits of tribal territory. For such communities, life itself was a dialogue with the natural world.

It is for this reason that many of the myths we encounter in this book blur the lines between human society and the natural world, often to the extent that they are indistinguishable. Animals – even plants and rocks – talk, think and act like humans, involving themselves in society as helpful participants,

Left: The picturesque Mount St Helens in Washington State. Being an active volcano, the mountain has attracted numerous myths and legends among the surrounding Native American peoples.

Above: Petroglyphs in Nine Mile Canyon in Utah show a hunt in progress, the Native American hunters using their bows against Desert Bighorn Sheep.

Far right: An Arapaho warrior, holding a highly decorated buffalo-hide shield plus a battle axe. The lavish shell beads indicate a person of high status in the tribe.

ambiguous tricksters and even outright enemies. Sometimes the human and natural world collide at a point of brutal intersection, as is seen in myths that reflect on the practice of hunting and killing creatures for survival. That many myths were spoken around this theme in particular is understandable to all those who have hunted. Killing, regardless of the social purpose or biological necessity, is a brutal business, robbing a creature of the life that, ultimately, is the only thing it truly possesses. Mythologizing such an act enables both the hunter and the prey to meet in a discussion, a place where human and animal can participate in an almost consensual dance of life.

The first myth we shall explore in this chapter is that of the Splinter-Foot Girl, an Arapaho narrative that charts the origins of buffalo hunting. As we shall see, it is much more than that, opening up a range of ideas and questions about the intersection between the natural world and the matters of society, life and death.

THE SPLINTER-FOOT GIRL (ARAPAHO)

One bleak and unrelenting winter, a party of Arapaho men were making their weary way through the wilderness looking for elk to hunt. On their way through scrubby land, one man cut open his leg on a thorny bush. The wound festered and became red and swollen, threatening the man's life. But then miraculously from the wound issued a female child, who instantly captured the hearts of the hardened men. Because of the nature of her origins, they called her the 'Splinter-Foot Girl', and tended to her gently and lovingly, sharing the burden of carrying her and making her cradles from sticks and panther skin.

THE NATURAL WORLD 73

At this time in history, the buffalo were not afraid of humans. Their chief was one Bone Bull, a mighty creature who kept a jealous eye upon his domain and the creatures in it. He came to hear of the existence of Splinter-Foot Girl and decided that he would marry her. So, following the custom of the time he sent out a magpie to ask the men for the girl's hand in marriage. The Arapaho warriors, who loved the girl and wanted to protect her, refused the request. The bird returned to Bone Bull, who was angered by the rejection. So he sent another more persuasive bird to repeat what was now a demand, but again it was turned down. Now Bone Bull's anger flared up and he sent the bird back again, this time with the message that Bone Bull himself would soon come for the girl by force if they did not consent. Still the humans refused. Only when Bone Bull sent the red 'Fire Owner'

Below: Major F.J. McCoy communicating with Arapaho chief Goes-In-Lodge through sign language. A rare few Westerners attempted to understand Native American culture.

bird, who conveyed the reality of Bone Bull's threat, did the warriors finally, with grievous reluctance, give in to the demands and prepared the young girl for marriage. Eventually they sent the girl away and she began her new, lonely life with Bone Bull, spending much of her time sitting beneath a long robe in the buffalo chief's lodge.

Yet time and regret gnawed at the warriors, and they realized that they had to rescue the girl from the clutches of Bone Bull. They enlisted the help of other creatures in the animal world to assist them, as their powers were not enough on their own. It was not easy to find such help, as Bone Bull was much feared throughout the animal kingdom. First the humans sent the flies, but Bone Bull shooed them away. Then they sent the magpie, but he was scared off. The courageous blackbird even went as far as alighting on Bone Bull's back, but even he was eventually driven away by the chief's bellow.

> BUT THE BLACKBIRD CAME BACK WITH A PLAN TO RESCUE SPLINTER-FOOT GIRL, A PLAN THAT REQUIRED THE SKILLS OF A MOLE AND A BADGER.

But the blackbird, a clever creature, came back with a plan to rescue Splinter-Foot Girl, a plan that required the skills of a mole and a badger. Now the girl sat beneath her robe in the same place in the buffalo's home on the earthen floor. Mole and badger dug a tunnel right up to the point at which the girl sat; the mole dug the initial tunnel, then the badger widened it sufficiently for a human to pass through. Eventually they revealed themselves to the girl and persuaded her to flee from Bone Bull, although it took much debate as the girl was very afraid of the great beast and knew that he would pursue her. Nevertheless, she eventually followed mole and badger back through the tunnel and was reunited with the menfolk. The warrior party then set off at speed across the land, hoping to escape from the vengeance of Bone Bull.

Knowing that the chief had greater physical strength than the humans, the warriors attempted to enlist the help of natural objects in their escape. First they asked a stone for help, but he replied: 'Bone Bull is too powerful, I cannot help you.'

Nevertheless, he permitted them to rest by his side before they continued on their way, their pace slowing as they tired from carrying the girl, who was now ill and had a severe cough. Then they came to a tree and asked him for help. The tree consented. He told the humans to run around him four times, then climb up high into his branches, resting in the fork that would be beyond the reach of Bone Bull and his mob.

Back in Bone Bull's camp, he finally discovered that the girl had been taken from him, and gathered his most fearsome warriors to set off in pursuit, using their horns to reveal and follow the tunnel dug by mole and badger. Eventually they reached the stone, and Bone Bull accused him of helping the humans. The stone denied it, but admitted that the people had rested in his shade. The buffalo chief then set off again following the trail, which led them to the tree. A drop of bloody sputum, coughed up by the girl, landed on a young buffalo calf resting at the base of the tree and revealed their presence. The buffalo gathered menacingly around the base of the tree.

The tree, however, was an ally of the humans and did not give in to Bone Bull's threats. (It is not uncommon in Native American myths for plants to take the side of humans in adversarial clashes between humankind and animals.) He taunted the buffalo, challenging them to bring him down with their immense strength and their horns. The buffalo therefore started to charge and ram the tree, starting with the youngest and the weakest and progressing up through the ranks of age, strength and stamina. But the tree had a plan. He knew that the impact at the end of each charge would break the buffalo's horns, despite the damage that was done to the trunk.

Above: A totemistic Native American tree carving in the Glacier Bay National Park, Alaska. Such carvings reconnected the viewer with ancestors, spirits and heroes.

Finally, Bone Bull stepped forward, his immense chest rising and falling in rage as he declared that he would be the one to bring the tree down. He charged from all points of the compass, but on his fifth attempt, taunted to fury by the tree, one of his horns stuck fast in the trunk. At this point, the tree told the warriors to use their bows and arrows, targeting the soft parts of Bone Bull at the back of his neck. So arrows rained down accurately and mercilessly, killing Bone Bull.

The rest of the buffalo were now humbled, their once lethal horns shortened and broken for perpetuity. Tree told them: 'Now your lives will be dominated by human beings. They will hunt and kill you, despite your horns, and you will be afraid of them. They will kill and eat you, and use your skins.' The buffalo heard the message and slunk away, destined to be the prey of human beings.

BACK IN BONE BULL'S CAMP, HE DISCOVERED THAT THE GIRL HAD BEEN TAKEN, AND GATHERED HIS MOST FEARSOME WARRIORS TO SET OFF IN PURSUIT.

Below: An Arapaho buffalo hunt. The hunter would attempt to fire his arrows down through the side of the chest, just above the front leg.

The myth of the Splinter-Foot Girl is an Arapaho rationalization of the origin of the buffalo hunt. Yet if we listen carefully to the narrative, this is not just a tale of victor and vanquished. Ultimately, the story is as much about negotiation as it is about strength, a negotiation in which many creatures and aspects of nature take their position and play their part. Although the buffalo are defeated in the struggle over the girl, there is no sense in which they are consigned to destruction, just that they now have to take their place within a new reality within nature. (This is in contrast to some of the Native American myths about the coming of the white man, which often recount the egregious destructive impulses of the newcomers, impulses that take no account of what depredations nature can sustain or tolerate.)

The outcome of such myths is a genuine resolution between nature and humans. The fact that animals, plants and natural features talk and behave like humans reiterates the closeness of the relationship between people and the natural world; everything is connected, so must ultimately reach some degree of reconciliation or accommodation.

Below: A painting on animal hide, from the hand of Plains Indians, shows a ceremonial dance following a buffalo hunt.

It should be noted that the account above is only really half of the Splinter-Foot Girl story. After the defeat of Bone Bull, the Round Rock also declares his desire to marry the girl. In essence, the saga the humans have just endured is then repeated, even to the extent of mole and badger having to rescue the girl again from the clutches of Round Rock. This part of the narrative illustrates how the negotiation with nature is always on-going and never completed.

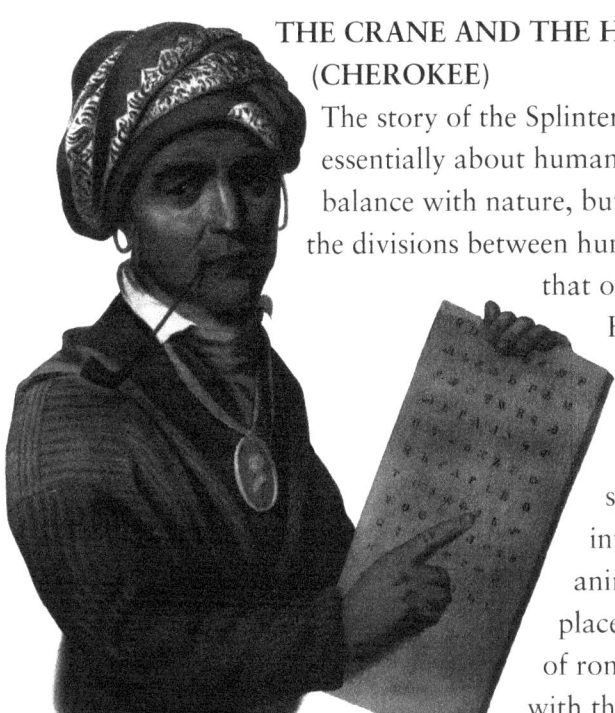

THE CRANE AND THE HUMMINGBIRD (CHEROKEE)

The story of the Splinter-Foot Girl is essentially about humanity achieving a balance with nature, but still preserving the divisions between human society and that of the creatures. However, many Native American myths blur the lines between species far more intimately. Often the animal characters are placed in some form of romantic interaction with the human beings, sometimes through mediums of disguise, often not. The openness of these relationships can appear strange to modern eyes, but to a culture that lives surrounded by nature itself, the romance serves as a metaphor for that continual respect for, and accommodation with, the creatures of land, water and air.

The Cherokee myth of the Crane and the Hummingbird is a good case in point. Here it is told by that great anthropologist of the Cherokee, James Mooney, who recorded a large number of their myths direct from their elders, reproducing the narratives in his *Myths of the Cherokee* from the *Nineteenth Annual Report of the Bureau of American Ethnology 1897–98, Part I.* (1900):

'The Hummingbird and the Crane were both in love with a pretty woman. She preferred the Hummingbird, who was as handsome as the Crane was awkward, but the Crane was so persistent that in order to get rid of him she finally told him he must challenge the other to a race and she would marry the winner. The Hummingbird was so swift – almost like a flash

Left: Cherokee chief Sequoyah, the man responsible for creating the Cherokee syllabary in the early 19th century, making the Cherokee language open to reading and writing.

Above: The ethnographer James Mooney (1861–1921) actually lived among the Cherokee tribe, hence became intimately acquainted with their mythology, and recorded many narratives for posterity.

Above: A Cherokee woman pictured c. 1930, opulently decorated with necklaces made from wampum beads.

of lightning – and the Crane so slow and heavy, that she felt sure the Hummingbird would win. She did not know the Crane could fly all night.

'They agreed to start from her house and fly around the circle of the world to the beginning, and the one who came in first would marry the woman. At the word, the Hummingbird darted off like an arrow and was out of sight in a moment, leaving his rival to follow heavily behind. He flew all day, and when evening came and he stopped to roost for the night he was far ahead. But the Crane flew steadily all night long, passing the Hummingbird soon after midnight and going on until he came to a creek and stopped to rest about daylight. The Hummingbird woke up in the morning and flew on again, thinking how easily he would win the race, until he reached the creek and there found the Crane spearing tadpoles, with his long bill, for breakfast. He was very much surprised and wondered how this could have happened, but he flew swiftly by and soon left the Crane out of sight again.

'The Crane finished his breakfast and started on, and when evening came he kept on as before. This time it was hardly midnight when he passed the Hummingbird asleep on a limb, and in the morning he had finished his breakfast before the other came up. The next day he gained a little more, and on the fourth day he was spearing tadpoles for dinner when the Hummingbird passed him. On the fifth and sixth days it was late in the afternoon before the Hummingbird came up, and on the morning of the seventh day the Crane was a whole night's travel ahead. He took his time at breakfast and then fixed himself up as nicely as he could at the creek and came in at the starting place where the woman lived, early in the morning. When the Hummingbird arrived in the afternoon he found he had lost the race, but the woman declared she would never have such an ugly fellow as the Crane for a husband, so she stayed single.'

The myth of the Crane and the Hummingbird is unashamedly humorous and phlegmatic. At its simplest, it provides a moral very much akin to that of the tortoise and the hare from *Aesop's Fables* along the lines of 'slow and steady wins the race'. The fact that the girl reneges on the bet and refuses to marry Crane because he is too ugly makes the point that people are people, after all, and not every pledge is honoured. Ultimately the Crane and Hummingbird are energetic and passing participants in the life of a bored girl, although it is notable that she stays single afterwards, living with the consequences of her choice.

> AT THE WORD, THE HUMMINGBIRD DARTED OFF LIKE AN ARROW AND WAS OUT OF SIGHT IN A MOMENT...

COYOTE AND FOX IN DISGUISE (NEZ PERCE)
The Nez Perce tribe occupy a territory in the Pacific Northwest on the Columbia River Plateau, far from the Cherokee. Like the Cherokee, however, their culture is replete with animal mythology, including humorous tales of almost slapstick romance in the animal kingdom. One standout example is that of the Coyote and the Fox and their attempts to find husbands in the Wolf Brothers. In this story, human beings are absent, although there are several morals of obvious relevance to the ethically aware.

Coyote spent his days hunting and preparing food, eking out his survival in a difficult wilderness. One day, in a low moment, he complained to his friend Fox about the hard and relentless nature of life, but he also proposed a solution. 'I need a husband to look after me, and to do all the hard work.' Fox looked

82 THE NATURAL WORLD

puzzled: 'But you are male, so it's impossible.' Coyote gave a wry smile: 'Ah, but I can pretend to be a woman.' Fox raised the natural objection that Coyote's true gender would be revealed in the bedroom, but Coyote dismissed this, saying he'd find a way around it. In this way he was able to persuade Fox to join him in the masquerade.

So Coyote and Fox began the transformation into women, dressing themselves in feminine clothing and contouring their bodies with padding. Thus disguised, they set out to flirt with the two Wolf Brothers, who happened to be looking for wives. Taken in by the seductive manner and attractive curves, the Wolf Brothers quickly decided that they would marry Fox and Coyote, with the Elder Brother proposing to Coyote and Younger Brother to Fox. Coyote, always one to seize the advantage, decided to test the two suitors before consenting to marriage. He set the Wolf Brothers a challenge – they had four days in which to hunt and bring Coyote and Fox a succulent banquet. Only if the standard of food was high enough would the marriages take place.

The Wolf Brothers, now galvanized by their romantic desire, consented to the proposal and set off on their hunt. For four days they stalked, chased, attacked and killed, collecting fine meats from many types of creature, from buffalo and elk through to goose and salmon, plus the juiciest selection of fruit and vegetables and the richest honey. Back at their camp, with Fox and Coyote lounging around indolently, the Wolf Brothers cooked up a magnificent feast and the duplicitous brides-to-be ate until they felt ill.

The four-day challenge had now passed, and the Wolf Brothers wanted their physical reward. Fox was naturally

Opposite: Hopi *kachina* dolls, depicting a cow (left) and wolf (right). Such dolls were traditionally carved from the roots of cottonwood trees.

Above: A fearsome carving of a wolf, from the Pacific Northwest coast. Some myths of this region regard wolves as the ancestors of human beings.

troubled by this, but Coyote had a plan. He pretended to head out into the bush to relieve himself, agreeing that once out of sight he would eventually cry 'Run!', and the two would make their break for freedom. On the way, he was distracted from his purpose and ended up climbing into the bed of the Wolf Brothers' mother, who woke in shock to find a cross-dressing Coyote becoming amorous. Her shrieks alarmed the whole village, and finally Coyote and Fox knew the game was up. They fled at speed, shedding their disguises as they went. Only after much running and hiding did Coyote and Fox escape their infuriated

WHY ANIMALS ARE THE WAY THEY ARE

THERE ARE MANY NATIVE American animal myths that explain the origins of the physical characteristics of creatures. For example, according to a myth from Washington State, Snail originally had large eyes with superb vision but naively lent them to Eagle, who decided that the eyes were so advantageous that he kept them. Snail therefore had to get by for the rest of time with tiny, poor-quality eyes on long stalks. A particularly vivid Iroquois tale tells the story of how Owl looked the way he did. The 'Everything-Maker' Raweno was creating animals, each one coming to him and making requests for certain characteristics. The rabbit, for example, wanted long legs like a deer. Raweno consented, stretching out the rabbit's hind limbs. But when he started work on the front legs he was interrupted by Owl, who made a long series of demands to make him the most beautiful bird in the world. Raweno, angered at the disruption, told Owl to turn away, as it was forbidden to

Left: A Pueblo boy with a tamed eagle poised on his arm. In Pueblo culture, eagles were often regarded as tribal guardians.

and humiliated pursuers. They declared that they would never try such a stunt again… but who knows if that was true.

The tale of Coyote and Fox's gender-crossing adventures might seem inconsequential and flippant, but it illustrates the breadth of Native American myths. We should always remind ourselves that these were oral traditions, stories brought to life in the act of telling around a campfire or while relaxing after a feast. While some myths could be achingly profound, others would be the equivalent of light entertainment, designed to make those listening laugh and unwind. What the animal kingdom provided watch the act of creation on other animals. But Owl disobeyed, and Raweno turned on him in a fury. He grabbed and shook Owl, an act that so terrified the bird that his eyes widened in shock and fright and stayed that way forever more. In an unforeseen consequence, Rabbit was so alarmed by witnessing Raweno's rage that he ran off before the Everything-Maker had a chance to stretch out his front legs, which is why Rabbit hops around to this day.

Another myth of animal characteristics is that told by the Brule Sioux about the Raven and why it is black in colour. Originally, Raven's feathers were a brilliant white. He sided with the buffalo against the humans, flying up high to spot hunters approaching, then warning the buffalo so that they could flee. The hunters, under the pressure of starvation, realized that they had to stop Raven. So one of the young hunters disguised himself as a buffalo and hid himself in the herd. One day when the hunters again approached, the Raven let out his alert and the buffalo fled, all except the disguised hunter. When the crow flew over this straggler to gather him up, the hunter grabbed him and tied his legs with a cord and attached the other end to a stone. The humans then debated what to do with the bird. One angry hunter simply grabbed Raven in vengeance and flung him, still attached to the cord and the stone, into a fire. The Raven's feathers were singed black, but his life was spared when the flames burnt through the cord and he was able to fly away, now forever darkened.

Left: From the Northwest coast of America, a ceremonial Native American spoon, with the handle carved in the form of a raven head.

was a ready cast of characters, each with understandable traits and characteristics. The wily natures of the Coyote and the Fox made them perfect for the parts played in the slapstick myth just recounted.

THE OWL GETS MARRIED (CHEROKEE)

As we have seen, the Native American intimacy with nature meant that the modern division between humans and the natural world largely did not exist. Indeed, such was the integration between nature and people that there are many tales of transformation of humans into animals and vice versa. Although some of these myths are intended for humorous effect, many others are tenderly profound and implicit commentaries on the interdependency of all creatures.

Below: A Zuni owl effigy. Although owls are often associated with death in Native American culture, they can also be wise and helpful to humans.

One such myth, that of the owl who got married, was again bestowed upon James Mooney during his anthropological journey through Cherokee lore in the 19th century:

'A widow with one daughter was always warning the girl that she must be sure to get a good hunter for a husband when she married. The young woman listened and promised to do as her mother advised. At last a suitor came to ask the mother for the girl, but the widow told him that only a good hunter could have her daughter. "I'm just that kind," said the lover, and again asked her to speak for him to the young woman. So the mother went to the girl and told her a young man had come a-courting, and as he said he was a good hunter she advised her daughter to take him. "Just as you say," said the girl. So when he came again the matter was all arranged, and he went to live with the girl.

'The next morning he got ready and said he would go out hunting, but before starting he changed his mind and said he would go fishing. He was gone all day and came home late at night, bringing only three small fish, saying that he had had no luck, but would have better success tomorrow. The next morning he started off again to fish and was gone all day, but came home at night with only two worthless spring lizards (*duwë'gä*) and the same excuse. Next day he said he would go hunting this time. He was gone again until night, and returned at last with only a handful of scraps that he had found where some hunters had cut up a deer.

'By this time the old woman was suspicious. So next morning when he started off again, as he said, to fish, she told her daughter to follow him secretly and see how he set to work. The girl followed through the woods and kept him in sight until he came down to the river, where she saw her husband change to a hooting owl (*uguku'*) and fly over to a pile of driftwood in the water and cry, "*U-gu-ku! hu! hu! u! u!*" She was surprised and very angry and said to herself, "I thought I had married a man, but my husband is only an owl". She watched and saw the owl look into the water for a long time and at last swoop down and bring up in his claws a handful of sand, from which he picked out a crawfish. Then he flew across to the bank, took the form of a man again, and started home with the crawfish. His wife hurried on ahead through the woods and got there before him. When he came in with the crawfish in his hand, she asked him where were all the fish he had caught. He said he had none, because an owl had frightened them all away. "I think you are the owl," said his wife, and drove him out of the house. The owl went into the woods and there he pined away with grief and love until there was no flesh left on any part of his body except his head.'

Above: A Dakota Sioux ghost dance shield features an owl in centre place. Owls were said to bring spiritual messages to this world from other spiritual dimensions.

The conclusion here is powerfully emotional. The message emerging from the tale seems to be that of a reflection on natural boundaries. Although we can, through an act of imagination, slip out of our frame and into that of another species, ultimately nature clamps down. To a large extent we are bound by the limits of biology, and that fact is both our strength and our tragedy.

INTO THIS WOMB-LIKE PLACE IADILLA WENT, HIS FATHER TELLING HIM THAT THE GOAL WAS TO SPEND 12 DAYS WITHOUT FOOD OR WATER.

OPECHEE THE ROBIN (CHIPPEWA)
Another example of a myth that involves a transformational shift between the human and animal world is the Chippewa legend of Opechee the Robin. The central figure of the myth is Iadilla, the adolescent son and only child of an old couple. Iadilla's father had ambitious plans for his son, wanting the boy to achieve greatness within his tribe, perhaps even becoming chief one day. To this end, the father wanted Iadilla to become connected with a great guardian spirit, one who would lead the boy to his natural ascendancy.

Iadilla's father looked to the sweat lodge – that sacred place of purification and insight – to bring about this spiritual advancement. He first led Iadilla to a secluded lodge in the nearby forest, in which Iadilla performed two purification rituals, moving between the sweltering and dark confines of the lodge and the

Below: A Chippewa scene hints at the encroaching Westernization of their culture by the European colonists.

rejuvenating chill waters of a nearby lake. But this was just the beginning of Iadilla's spirit quest. Once the purification was completed, his father then led him even deeper into the wood to another sweat lodge, located in silent isolation away from all human contact. Into this womb-like place Iadilla went, his father telling him that the goal was to spend 12 days without food or water. Only through such an act of endurance would a great and strong guardian spirit come to him, despite the threat the challenge posed to his life. Iadilla anxiously entered the sweat lodge on the first day of his journey, his father promising that he would come back every day to offer words of encouragement and support, as well as to tend the heated stones.

The days wore on, and Iadilla lay silently in the lodge. After a week without food or water, his strength – both spiritual and physical – began to fail him. He became painfully thin and crazed with thirst, fearful for his life. When his father returned to the lodge and spoke to him from the outside, Iadilla expressed his fears: 'Father, I am no longer strong enough to continue this quest. My body is ill and my dreams are plagued with visions of suffering and evil. Please give me your permission to break my fast.'

But Iadilla's father let ambition override paternal love, and refused permission to end the fast. He sternly advised Iadilla to endure further, so that he could reap the rewards in life and bring his parents what would be their last chance of glory. Iadilla grimly consented and continued with his silent purgatory.

The boy's physical decline continued, and as he entered day 11 of the fast he once again implored his father to release him from his obligation. His father snapped back angrily. 'You have only one more day left. Tomorrow I will come to you bearing a large meal to restore your strength – we are preparing the food now. Do not bring shame down upon this family by giving up now.' Iadilla, now barely conscious and unable to move, felt the pang of guilt and resumed his vigil.

Above: The Chippewa chief Pee-Che-Kir. He holds a pipe, which was used for a broad range of ceremonies and rituals, from invoking the bonds between heaven and earth to formalizing peace treaties.

Far right: A painted buffalo skull, of a type used in Plains Indian camp circle ceremonies or in Blackfoot sweat lodge rituals.

Morning broke on day 12 and Iadilla's father awoke overjoyed. He gathered up the food his wife had prepared and hurried out to the sweat lodge. As he approached, however, he heard Iadilla's voice from within, strong but with a bitter commitment: 'My father has destroyed me as a man. He would not listen to my pleas, and has pushed me beyond my strength. It shall be his loss, however. I shall be forever happy in my new state, as I have shown obedience to my parents. He will suffer for

THE SWEAT LODGE

THE SWEAT LODGE IS a distinctive space in Native American spirituality, a dark and hot world in which the senses are refined and heightened, visions and spirits visit, and the body is purified. Physically, the sweat lodge is essentially a small wikiup lodge, the frame made from flexible branches or saplings, bent upwards to a central point some 1.2–1.5m (4–5ft) above the ground, with the diameter of the whole structure roughly 3m (10ft) across. The coverings applied to enclose the lodge varied, but included buffalo hides, bear skins and other furs, as well as thick layers of leafy branches or sods of earth. Whatever the material, the lodge becomes a dark, silent and insulated place, the only light coming, temporarily when opened, from the entrance; the entrance traditionally faced east, so that the participants could greet the rising sun each day.

The sweat lodge ceremony is an involved one, with variations according to each tribe and local tradition. In summary, an individual or several people go into the lodge, entering willingly to undergo a spirit quest, typically seeking purification of body and soul, as well as spiritual direction. (The participant has often undergone a prior period of fasting for further cleansing effect.) The person sits inside the lodge, leaning against one wall. A fire is lit outside, with stones heated until they are red hot. At the right moment, the sweat lodge keeper transfers the stones, brushed of embers, into the lodge, stacking them in the centre, before closing the flap of the entrance tightly. There, in the darkness and the rising heat, the participant undergoes his purification. As his body sweats, he sees visions and receives messages from the spirit world. If there are multiple people within the lodge, they may take it in turns to recount and interpret their visions to each other. This process might go on for many hours, or, more traditionally, some days. Although the sweat lodge can be physically uncomfortable, it also in many ways is meant to represent the womb, a place of safety, restoration and rebirth.

his actions, for my guardian spirit has made a just decision. He has shown me pity in another way, by giving me another shape. Now I must go.'

Iadilla's father, concerned by the words he was hearing, pushed back the hides covering the entrance to the sweat lodge and saw Iadilla sat up, having painted his chest and shoulders a deep red colour. The father burst inside, shouting out: 'My son, my son, do not leave me!' But it was too late, for at that

Above: The exposed frame of a sweat lodge, with the hot stone pile in the centre. When covered with foliage, the lodge would form a dark, hot, womb-like world of contemplation and visions.

Above: A Chippewa wedding ceremony under way. As in Western wedding ceremonies, the bride and groom exchange vows, scripted by ancient traditions.

moment Iadilla was transformed into a red-breasted robin. He flew up quickly and alighted upon the ridgepole of the tent, even as his old father let out an anguished cry of loss. Seeing and pitying his father's distress, Iadilla – now Opechee the Robin – spoke words of reassurance: 'Do not grieve, father, for I shall be so much happier as a bird, free from human pain and sorrow. I will cheer your spirits with my bird song. Having been hungry, now I shall get my food so easily, taking it from the mountains and in the fields. Once I was thirsty, but now I shall drink sweet dew and the water of little springs. Once I trudged through difficult forest paths, but now I fly through pathways in the bright, clear air, free from thorns and branches. Goodbye, my father! I am so happy!'

With these words, Iadilla took flight up and out of the sweat lodge, and up into the bright blue sky. Yet he never forgot his loyalty or affection for his parents. He built his nest close to his father's lodge, so that every day his father could emerge into the morning light and call out 'Opechee! Opechee!' And Opechee would sing sweetly in return.

THE ORIGIN OF THE MOSQUITO (TLINGIT)

Another strand of nature myth within Native American traditions is origin narratives: essentially, how animals came to be in the first place. As we have already seen, often such myths centre around an act of a divine (albeit fallibly human) creator figure.

Left: A traditional Tlingit actor's mask worn during story telling. Native American mythology thrived through the narrative talent and theatricality of the teller.

94 THE NATURAL WORLD

On other occasions, however, creatures are brought into being in a moment of physical rupture or violence, bursting into the world as the unintended outcome of a human act. A good example is the Tlingit myth of how the mosquito arrived in the world.

In ancient times, humans used to be the prey of a huge and hideous giant. He would hunt down, kill and eat the people, snacking with relish on the heart, his favourite part of the prey. The humans discussed ways in which they could kill the giant, and one brave warrior suggested a solution. He went out into the giant's territory and lay on the ground, pretending to be dead. The giant came along, saw the body on the ground and laughed. 'Look at how easy it is for me to feast on humans. Now they just die in front of me out of fear, ready for me to eat.' Feeling that the human body was still warm, the giant flung it over his shoulder and carried it back to his lair.

> AS QUICK AS A FLASH, THE WARRIOR SWUNG HIS KNIFE DOWN AND INTO THE GIANT'S LEFT HEEL, PIERCING THE HEART WITHIN.

The warrior was alone in the lair as the giant went out to collect firewood. But then the giant's son, much smaller than his father, entered the lodge, at which point the warrior leapt up, grabbed him and held a knife to his throat. 'Tell me where your father's heart is, so that I can kill him', demanded the warrior. The terrified young giant broke down: 'It is in his left heel.' At that moment, the great giant entered the lodge once again. As quick as a flash, the warrior swung his knife down and into the giant's left heel, piercing the heart within. The giant let out a piteous cry, and as he fell and lay dying, shouted out: 'You have killed me, but I will keep feasting on humans forever.' The warrior, unnerved by the giant's final curse, cut the body into tiny pieces and threw them onto the fire to ensure he was dead. Once the body was reduced to ash, the warrior then took the remains outside and scattered them into the blowing wind. Yet as the motes of ash swirled in the air, each tiny piece was transformed into a mosquito. Floating on the breeze, the warrior then heard the giant's voice once more, saying 'I will feast on your flesh forever.' At that moment, the warrior felt the bite of the mosquito, which began to draw his blood.

Far left: A drawing of a Tlingit warrior, armed with a bow and arrow and wearing basic body armour, made from strips of wood or ivory.

Far right: Four members of the Coast Salish people – native to the Pacific Northwest coast – as seen c. 1921. Western clothes have already taken over from traditional dress.

THE BRIDGE OF THE GODS (PUYALLUP)

Tribal landscapes are sacred places. Contours, mountains, rivers, woodland, even distinctive rocks and trees all have their place in Native American mythology. As we saw in the creation stories of Chapter 1, tribal regions are circumscribed places with boundaries set by oceans, mountains, forests and rivers, and the world beyond is a vague place, strange and imbalanced.

Myths are ways in which geographical explanations are provided, and sense made of a world that, without such narratives, would be shapeless and threatening. We can see how mythology can 'map' a landscape spiritually in the story of The Bridge of the Gods, hailing from the Puyallup tribe of the Pacific Northwest, centred in Washington State.

So the legend goes, at one time in history a huge rockslide poured down into the Colorado River near Cascade Locks, the rocks piling up until they formed a natural bridge over the river. This became a sacred site known as Tamanawas Bridge, or Bridge of the Gods, for in its centre burned a sacred fire, the only fire in the world. Humans travelled from every point of the compass to source fire for themselves, taking back smouldering embers.

Watching over the fire was one Loowitlatkla ('Lady of Fire') – or Loowit for short – an old woman who diligently tended the flames. A great local chief called Tyee Sahale wanted to express his gratitude to Loowit, and decided to bestow on her the gift of eternal life, a gift that he had already granted to his two sons Klickitat and Wyeast. Yet the gift of eternal life was not welcomed by Loowit, for she was old and tired and had no desire to live forever. Unfortunately, Tyee Sahale was unable to retract the gift once given, and so offered to grant her one wish by way of compensation. Loowit chose to be young and beautiful. Thus transformed, she became known as one of the most attractive women in the world.

But here were planted the seeds of trouble. Klickitat and Wyeast, travelling from afar to see the renowned beauty for themselves, both fell in love with Loowit. Their competition for

> YET THE GIFT OF ETERNAL LIFE WAS NOT WELCOMED BY LOOWIT, FOR SHE WAS OLD AND TIRED AND HAD NO DESIRE TO LIVE FOREVER.

THE NATURAL WORLD 97

HE BROUGHT DOWN THE BRIDGE OF THE GODS, AND IT CRASHED DOWN INTO THE COLORADO RIVER, WHERE THE WATER STILL BOILS AND FROTHS TO THIS DAY.

her love flared into outright war, with whole regions laid waste by violence and destruction. Tyee Sahale watched, his sadness eventually flaring into a raging anger. Using his powers, he brought down the Bridge of the Gods, and it crashed down into the Colorado River where the water still boils and froths to this day. In the ultimate act of vengeance, however, he turned Loowit, Klickitat and Wyeast into mountains, the crags springing up where the hapless humans fell. Loowit became what is today known as Mount St Helens, the symmetrical proportions

Right: Mount Adams, the mythical manifestation of Klickitat, turned into the mountain by Tyee Sahale in an act of vengeance and anger at human failures.

of the mountain and its glistening snows reflecting Loowit's beauty. Wyeast became Mount Hood, while Klickitat was transformed into Mount Adams, the towering bulk of these peaks forever reminders of the destructive nature of unrequited love.

In many other stories in this book we will see nature at play, being both stage and characters in the spiritual drama. The intimacy with nature is surely one of the reasons why Native American mythology resonates so strongly with an urban and noisy modern age. Within the myths and legends, we sense a time when people peacefully played their part in the unfolding of the natural world and did not stand separate from it.

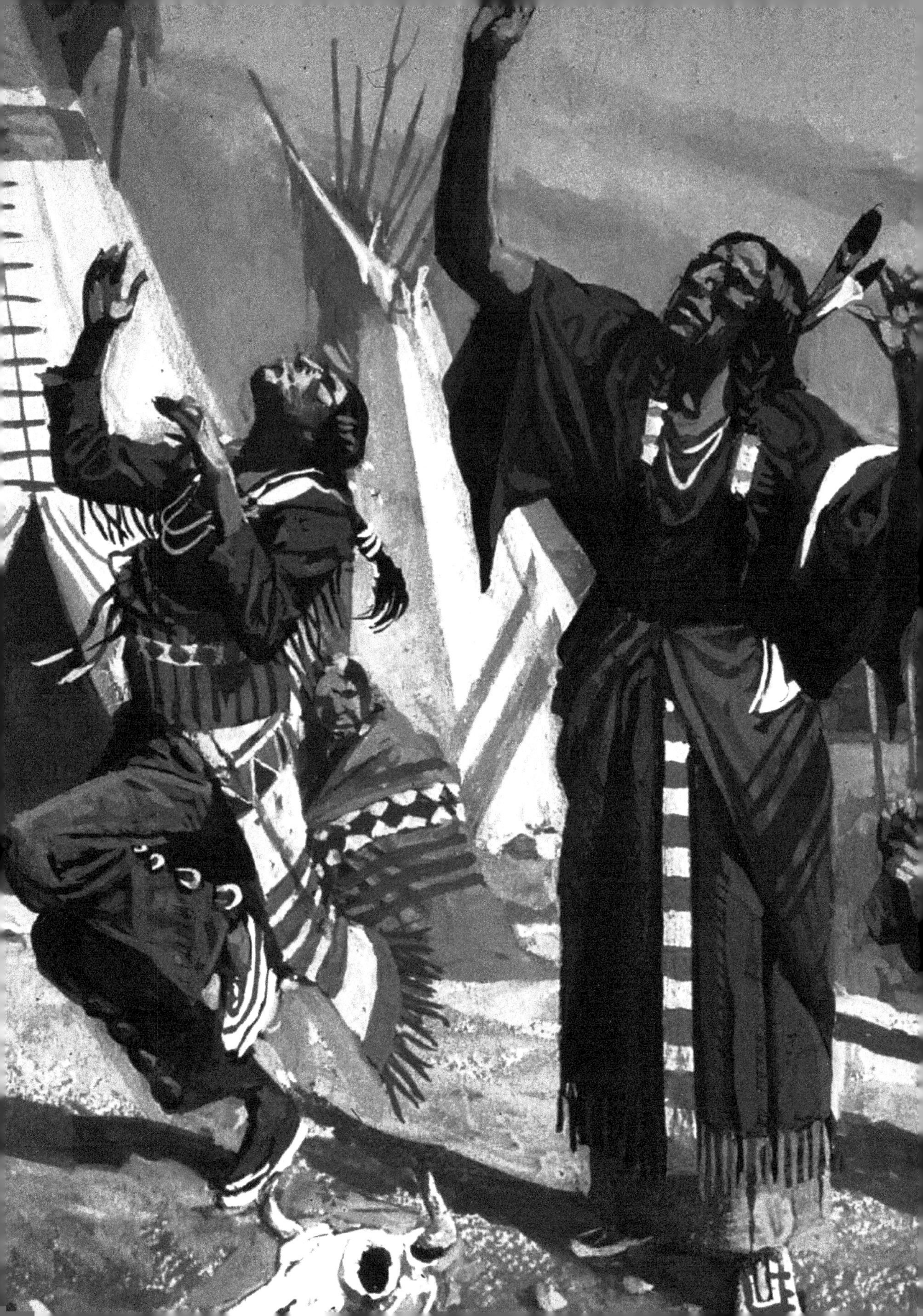

4

GHOSTS, SPIRITS AND THE DEAD

In the Christian religion, the world of spirits is a definable place, a realm – heavenly or otherwise – to which the souls of the dead migrate, distinct from the physical shell of the body that held them during their lives. Communication between the two realms is difficult. The spirit realm and the human realm are related, but are essentially other worlds entirely.

From Native American myths and legends, it is far trickier to build any sort of overarching doctrine about the other world, based on the numerous narratives of human encounters with ghosts and spirits. Across the tribes of North America, there is a near-universal sense of a spiritual realm, a place of disembodied – or temporarily embodied – spirits that interact with the living.

But unlike the Christian tradition, the spirit realm is often not distinct from the physical, but rather is laced through it like a fragrant scent wafting in warm summer air. Beyond the recognition that there is a spiritual dimension alongside existence,

Left: Two members of a Sioux tribe perform the ghost dance. The dance would summon the spirits of ancestors, who would work and fight on behalf of the living.

there is little uniformity across all the tribal traditions. Some have clear beliefs in an afterlife, while others believe that death is the emphatic end of everything. Of those tribes that believe in the afterlife, some see us as having one soul, which simply replicates the person we were in life, while others see us with multiple souls, each linked to a certain place, object or act of migration. Ghosts and spirits can be welcome messengers, loyally guiding people with their insight from the spirit world, or they can be frightening harbingers of doom. Spirits can also be embodied at times, the physical manifestations ranging across all forms of humanity and nature.

The permutations and divisions go on, cumulatively creating spirit worlds as diverse, populous and frenetic as our own. The myths and legends that follow revolve around what happens when these two worlds connect and slip through one another, often with unintended consequences.

Above: A Pawnee ghost dance shirt. The shirts themselves were regarded as imbued with spiritual power and protection for the wearer.

MONDAWMIN (CHIPPEWA/OJIBWA)

The myth of a human individual wrestling with a divine spirit is an old one, featuring in religious traditions across the globe. In the Native American context, it is a theme that emerges poignantly in the myth of Mondawmin, the Corn Spirit, told by the tribes in the northeastern parts of the United States. The importance of this myth highlights the importance of corn itself to many Native American tribes – those who could grow it, and thus establish developed and dependable agriculture, could free themselves from the unpredictable food cycles involved with hunting and gathering. In our time of plentiful food, it is hard to understand the importance of such a step culturally and philosophically, and the psychological reassurance it provided.

This particular myth begins in a far-off time, and is centred, as it so often is, around a Native American family: a man, his wife and his several children. Much of the family's time was spent hunting or collecting food. The father would head out early in the morning and spend his day tracking, hunting and fishing. His wife and children, meanwhile, would be equally industrious collecting fruits, vegetables and other edible plants. Between them they managed to scratch out an existence, especially during the plentiful summer months. During the wintertime, however, both edible flora and fauna were scarce, the landscape locked beneath snow and ice.

Below: A Chippewa/Ojibwa family gather around the campfire. The Chippewa's main industries were fur trading and maple syrup harvesting.

104 GHOSTS, SPIRITS AND THE DEAD

Over time, the family's eldest son approached adulthood and soon he would be able to help his father hunt through the forests around him. But first he had to embark on a spirit quest, a seven-day fast in which he hoped that he would meet his spirit guide who would show him the path of his life.

So the son went out into the forest on his own, building a rudimentary hut in which he would live during his fast. While out in the forest, and with hunger steadily loosening his grip on rational thought, he wandered far and wide, observing the natural world around him. During his ruminations, he noticed how wonderful and bounteous nature could be. He saw clearly the multitude of insects swirling in the air. He observed the animals of different kinds and contrasting mannerisms, from the hopping humble rabbit to the mighty roaring bear and the fast-running deer. He gazed up at the birds of the sky, swooping and soaring above him. Around his feet grew a harvest of plant life, while above him towered the majestic forest trees, stretching out their boughs, leaves and branches into the blue summer sky that capped the heavens. In the rivers and lakes he perceived the swirling, bubbling lives of the fish and other aquatic creatures beneath the surface.

Yet at the same time as he saw fertility and beauty in nature, he was also profoundly aware of how hard that world was during the cruel winter months, when animals hid, hibernated or died, when plants shrivelled and rotted, when lakes and rivers froze over, and when the sky filled with snow or icy rain. At all such moments of recognition, he looked towards the heavens and spoke the prayer: 'Master of Life, help my people.' More than anything, he longed for a guiding spirit to come to him, one that would show him the secrets of how to hunt and gather food during the inhospitable seasons. With such knowledge, he would truly be able to support his family.

On the fourth day of his fast the boy was becoming weak, his mind dreamy, fitful and wandering, reality a crumbling illusion.

Far left: May-maush-kow-aush, the chief medicine man of the Chippewa, and his family – wife, and daughter Helen – seen here in a photograph taken in 1900.

WITH HUNGER STEADILY LOOSENING HIS GRIP ON RATIONAL THOUGHT, HE WANDERED FAR AND WIDE, OBSERVING THE NATURAL WORLD AROUND HIM.

Above: Wunzh wrestles with the spirit-being, fighting through his physical weakness and thereby receiving the gift of corn from Mondawmin.

As the sun was setting, however, there was a burst of light from the sky and a figure was seen descending – a young, handsome man dressed in beautiful green and yellow clothes with an ornate headdress made of feathers. The figure reached Earth and then walked forward and addressed the boy: 'The Master of Life has observed you and has heard your prayers. He sees how in your heart you wish to help your people, and be worthy of them. He is also pleased that you seek to make your life great through peace, not war. I have come to help you realize your wishes. First, I will bestow upon you your spirit name – it is to be Wunzh!'

Now the spirit gave Wunzh the most surprising message of all. 'If you wish to help your people, first you must wrestle with me.' Wunzh was alarmed by the request as he felt so weak from his fasting. But he summoned up all his strength and engaged in combat with the strange spirit, each trying to defeat the other. After a while, just as Wunzh was about to give up from weakness, the spirit broke away. 'That is enough for now,' he announced, 'but I will be back tomorrow to resume our fight'. And with that, he ascended back into the heavens.

For two more days the spirit returned as promised to fight the ever-weakening Wunzh, who wondered what would happen if the spirit beat him in combat, an outcome that felt inevitable given his deteriorating physical condition. Yet on the sixth day, after the wrestling the spirit made an unexpected announcement. 'Tomorrow we will wrestle for the last time, as the Master of Life has decided to grant your wishes. When we fight, you will defeat and kill me. When you see that I am dead, find a place in the earth that is soft and clear of roots and bury me there, covering me with my clothes. Tend to my grave carefully, keeping it free from weeds and grasses. When you do this, you will receive the insight you desire.'

And so on the seventh day, Wunzh prepared to wrestle for the last time. Early in the morning, his father came to him with food as it was the last day of the fast, but Wunzh refused it, knowing that he must remain pure for this last battle. His father went away, unaware of the struggle in which Wunzh was locked.

The spirit returned as promised at sunset, and the two fought together for the last time. All was fulfilled as predicted. Wunzh, summoning his final vestiges of strength, killed the spirit and buried him as required. Then Wunzh returned to his village, not telling his family about the events in the forest, but secretly sneaking out to tend to the spirit's grave.

FOR TWO MORE DAYS THE SPIRIT RETURNED AS PROMISED TO FIGHT THE EVER-WEAKENING WUNZH.

Below: An Ojibwa family photographed in their wigwam. Wigwams often had a domed construction, distinguishing them from the Plains Indian tipi.

The days and weeks passed, with spring giving way to summer. Then, at the height of the season when all of nature was at its most fertile, Wunzh led his father to the spirit's grave and there told his father of all that had occurred during his fast. But at the gravesite, standing proud and tall, was a beautiful corn plant, its long stem, yellow kernels and green leaves all resplendent in the summer sun. Wunzh took off an ear of corn and gave it to his father. 'This is a gift from my guardian spirit. His name is Mondawmin, meaning "corn for all Indians". This is the answer to my questions. For with this plant, and its crop, we will have a source of food that does not depend upon our hunting and gathering. During the autumn months we will harvest its crop, and this will be stored throughout the winter, ensuring that we have plentiful food during the cold, hard months. This is Mondawmin's gift to all of humanity'.

As well as the gift of corn, Wunzh also received the wisdom of how to sow, tend, harvest, strip and cook the corn plant, a knowledge that he passed on to his family and through them to all Native American people.

Below: The Cherokee leader David Vann (1800–63), a man of both European and Native American blood who acted as a Cherokee treasurer and negotiator.

THE *NUNNE'HI* (CHEROKEE)

The story of Mondawmin is a poetic vision of the origins of corn. Like so many Native American myths, it sees a natural product as a gift, something to be treated with reverence and celebration for what it means to those who use it, and whose survival may depend on it. There are other legends in which tribal people are given salvation in the form of assistance from the spirit world. A resonant example is that of the *Nunne'hi*, or immortals. According to Cherokee mythology, they are a race of spirit people who live high up in the mountains. Although they are spirit beings, they live much as humans do in villages and townhouses, with all the social trappings. Anthropologist James Mooney also noted that: 'They were invisible excepting when they wanted to be seen, and then they looked and spoke just like other Indians. They were very fond of music and dancing, and hunters in the mountains would often hear the dance, songs and the drum beating in some invisible townhouse, but when they went toward the sound it would shift about and they would hear it behind them or away in some other direction, so that they could never find the place where the dance was. They were a friendly people, too, and often brought lost wanderers to their townhouses under the mountains and cared for them there until they were rested and then guided them back to their home.' This friendliness extended to being a protector to tribal people against those that threatened them with violence.

Nowhere is this last trait better displayed than in the story of the defence of the Nikwasi. This myth was beautifully rendered by James Mooney during his research among the Cherokee:

'Long ago a powerful unknown tribe invaded the country from the southeast, killing people and destroying settlements wherever they went. No leader could stand against them, and in a little while they had wasted all the lower settlements and advanced into the mountains. The warriors of the old town of Nikwasi, on the head of Little Tennessee, gathered their wives and children into the townhouse and kept scouts constantly on the lookout for the presence of danger. One morning just before daybreak the spies saw the enemy approaching and at once gave the alarm. The Nikwasi men seized their arms and rushed out to meet the attack, but after a long, hard fight they found themselves overpowered and began to retreat, when suddenly a stranger stood among them and shouted to the chief to call off his men and he himself would drive back the enemy. From the dress and language of the stranger the Nikwasi people thought him a chief who had come with

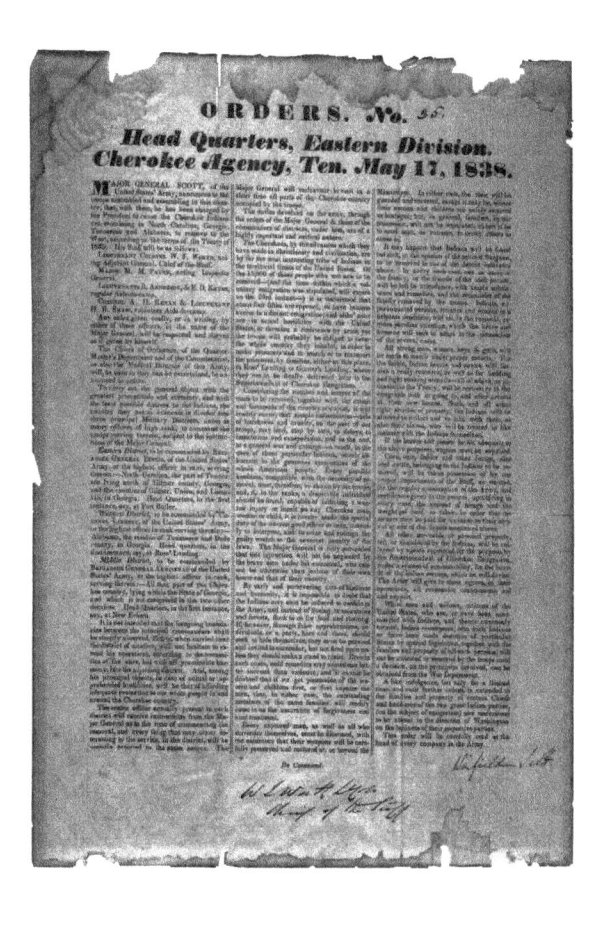

Above: The Indian Removal Bill announces the US Army's enforcement of the Indian Removal Act against Cherokee tribes of the east coast, 1838.

Above: An artist's depiction of the 'Trail of Tears', the brutal forced relocation of Native American tribes by the colonizers between 1831 and 1850.

reinforcements from the Overhill settlements in Tennessee. They fell back along the trail, and as they came near the townhouse they saw a great company of warriors coming out from the side of the mound as through an open doorway. Then they knew that their friends were the *Nunne'hi*, the Immortals, although no one had ever heard before that they lived under Nikwasi mound.

'The *Nunne'hi* poured out by hundreds, armed and painted for the fight, and the most curious thing about it all was that they became invisible as soon as they were outside of the settlement, so that although the enemy saw the glancing arrow or the rushing tomahawk, and felt the stroke, he could not see who sent it. Before such invisible foes the invaders soon had to retreat, going first south along the ridge to where it joins the main ridge, which separates the French Broad from the Tuckasegee, and then turning with it to the northeast. As they retreated they tried to shield themselves behind rocks and trees, but the *Nunne'hi* arrows went around the rocks and killed them from the other side, and they could find no hiding place. All along the ridge they fell, until when they reached the head of Tuckasegee not more than half a dozen were left alive, and in despair they sat down and cried out for mercy. Ever since then the Cherokee have called the place Dayulsun'yi, "Where they cried". Then the *Nunne'hi* chief told them they had deserved their punishment for attacking a peaceful tribe, and he spared their lives and told them to go home and take the news to their people. This was the Indian custom, always to spare a few to carry back the news of defeat. They went home toward the north and the *Nunne'hi* went back to the mound.

'And they are still there, because, in the last war, when a strong party of Federal troops came to surprise a handful of Confederates posted there they saw so many soldiers guarding the town that they were afraid and went away without making an attack.'

Below: Stand Watie (1806–71) was a Cherokee leader who also served as a commander in the Confederate States Army during the American Civil War, rising to the rank of brigadier general.

THE *NUNNE'HI* POURED OUT BY HUNDREDS, ARMED AND PAINTED FOR THE FIGHT...

Given the point in history at the end of the 19th century, there is something painfully tender about this narrative. By this stage of Native American history, most of the tribal lands had been absorbed, often violently (bordering on, or literally, genocide in some areas) by the march of the white people across the American continent. The belief in a race of spirit protectors, therefore, seems indicative of both a pained wistfulness but also, potentially, a source of future strength – the guardianship of the *Nunne'hi* may come from spiritual warfare. The comment Mooney recorded about their presence during the American Civil War (1861–65) suggests that, to the Cherokee of that time, they were a latent force that could one day step forward again to provide salvation. Whatever the modern-day interpretation is, the myth of the *Nunne'hi* is deeply poetic and shows just how tangibly the spirit world could intervene in the affairs of humans.

BLUE JAY AND IOI (CHINOOK)

The Chinook people of the northwest Pacific have some of the most potent, entertaining and profound of the Native American mythologies relating to ghosts and spirits. As with many similar mythologies, in the Chinook tales the boundaries between the dead and the living are broken down, with the world of the dead becoming accessible to the world of the living. Family relationships, even romances, therefore survived the grave with consequences at times amusing, and at other times tragic.

One of the most extensive and compelling of these ghost narratives is the Chinookan legend of Blue Jay and Ioi. Blue Jay was the name of a young man, so called because his character reflected that of the trickster bird, and he lived with his sister Ioi. Now Ioi's life was very hard, a constant round of cooking, cleaning and labouring in the fields. So Ioi spoke to Blue Jay and told him to find an old wife from among the dead who could be brought back to life to help her in her duties. With relish, Blue Jay agreed to the request. Yet instead of finding an old spirit, he took himself a beautiful young bride, a chieftain's daughter who had only been dead for one day. Angered by his choice but accepting it, Ioi told Blue Jay to journey to the land of the Supernatural People where they could restore his spirit wife to physical existence.

So the impetuous Blue Jay journeyed down into the underworld with his wife until he arrived at the small town inhabited by the Supernatural People. He asked them to bring his spirit-wife back to life, but they refused, saying that instead Blue Jay had to travel to the town that restored people who had only been dead for one day. So Blue Jay and his wife continued

Above: Haunting pictographs of ghosts and spectral beings seen in the Great Gallery, Horseshoe Canyon, in the Canyonlands National Park, Utah.

onwards, walking for another whole day until they arrived at the right town. Yet again, Blue Jay's request was denied, because by the time that they arrived in the town his wife had been dead for two days, not one. The Supernatural People pointed him in the direction of the town that restored people who had been dead for two days. So on the couple trudged, but when they arrived a day later at the next town, his wife was now three days dead, and thus one day too old to be restored in the two days' dead town.

Thus Blue Jay and his wife became trapped in a pattern, always arriving at the next town of restoration one day too late. Eventually, on the fifth day, the Supernatural People overlooked the protocols and turned Blue Jay's spirit-wife into a living person once again. Yet Blue Jay had grown somewhat accustomed to life in the spirit world and decided to stay there for a while. The Supernatural People took him into their community and soon he rose in status and popularity until he was eventually made a chief. Yet with the passage of time, Blue Jay steadily began to crave the things of the land of the living, and thus returned.

The arrival of Blue Jay and his new wife had a series of unforeseen consequences. The bereaved chief came to hear that his daughter was back from the dead, and that she was married to Blue Jay. While her return brought the chief joy, he was less than enamoured that she had wed the disreputable Blue Jay. The chief sent a messenger to him, telling him that in return for his daughter's hand in marriage Blue Jay would have to give him his hair as a gift. Blue Jay chose the least mature of his response options and simply ignored the message. The chief was thus angered and assembled a party of warriors to go to find Blue Jay and settle the matter.

Above: This artwork, created in the 1890s, vividly conveys the frenetic passion and physical energy of the ghost dance ritual, as the participants bring forth the spirits of the dead.

Blue Jay saw the hostile crowd coming and took avoidance to new levels by transforming himself into the bird of his name and flying away. At this turn of events his wife passed out from shock, collapsing to the ground unconscious. She remained that way permanently in Blue Jay's absence, with search parties going out frantically to try to find him, as only his return would bring her back to herself. Yet Blue Jay did not come back, and eventually she passed away once more and her spirit made its final journey to the Land of the Souls.

Below: A moving portrait of a Chinook mother and child. The contraption around the infant was designed to flatten the head, for aesthetic and cultural reasons.

The myth of Blue Jay and his spirit wife is just part of a saga of stories involving the mischievous man. Blue Jay becomes a prankster of both the realm of the living and of the spirits, causing problems in each sphere. In a later part of the story, the theme of the quest for a wife is reversed when a group of spirits from the Ghost World – also known as the 'Shadow-land' – ventured up into the world above, looking for wives among the still-living. One of them spotted Ioi and fell in love with her. Ioi was captivated by this ethereal visitor, so after the ghost had presented her with wedding gifts, he took her back down to the Ghost World to live.

When the village discovered that Ioi had gone there was much lamentation, but although it was suspected that she had been taken to the Ghost World, no one knew how to get there. Eventually, after a year, Blue Jay made it his quest to go to find Ioi. He set out, asking all the animals around him to direct him to the Ghost World, but they either did not know or would not say. Eventually, however, he found someone who did know the route and guided Blue Jay to the Ghost World in return for money.

Thus Blue Jay found himself once more in the realm of spirits. It was a barren and cold place, full of the bones of people and creatures who once were. Eventually he found Ioi, but she was sitting amid a pile of bones – these, apparently, were her in-laws. As Blue Jay discovered, the spirits who inhabited the Ghost World were highly acoustically sensitive. For much of the time they would be assembled, their bones taking up human appearance, but as soon as a loud noise was made they would collapse back into scattered bones again.

> THIS FACT WAS DELIGHTFUL TO THE PRANKSTER BLUE JAY, AS HE HAD THE POWER TO REDUCE PEOPLE TO BONES WITH JUST A LOUD SHOUT.

This fact was delightful to the prankster Blue Jay, as he had the power to reduce people to bones with just a loud shout. One time, while fishing with his ghostly brother-in-law on a dead lake in a rotting boat, he kept intermittently shouting, turning his fishing companion into a pile of bones on several occasions. Furthermore, when people were in this state he enjoyed mixing up the bones to create physiological chaos when they returned to human form – adults with children's heads, for example. He was not making himself popular, to say the least.

Yet, as with his journey to the land of the Supernatural People, Blue Jay steadily grew tired of his surroundings. When he went fishing again, for example, he was disheartened by the way that all they appeared to catch were horrible-looking bones, even though in the Ghost World these bones were regarded as prime catches. Therefore, when Ioi came up with a plan to send him back to the human world, her words fell on receptive ears. Ioi told Blue Jay, truthfully, that in the world above five fires were raging on the prairies, and that he was needed there to put them out. To accomplish this feat, she would give him five magical pots of water. It was important, she explained, that he only use one pot of water for each fire.

Blue Jay embraced the mission, but less so his sister's explicit instructions. When he found the fires, he used more water on the first four than he was supposed to, so by the time he reached the fifth fire he had no means of putting out the flames. The conflagration raged larger and larger until it engulfed Blue Jay, killing him and sending him back down to the Ghost World as a permanent resident.

The problem was that Blue Jay did not recognize that he was dead, which was apparently common with those who are recently deceased. Ioi told him time and again of the truth, but he gave his customary reply: 'Ioi is always telling lies.' Because he did not believe that he was dead, he did not see the Ghost World with the eyes of a dead man. Thus the bones fished from the lake still looked like skeletons to him, rather than the fine fish seen by the rest of the ghosts around him. Blue Jay tried his old trick of shouting to get those around him to collapse into piles of bones, but his ghost-voice no longer carried this power. Even the medicine men of the Ghost World were unable to help him, and shooed him away when he sought their counsel and assistance. Eventually Blue Jay went mad, unable to adjust his spirit to the life of the dead.

The story of Blue Jay's descent into the Ghost World is salutary. It contains an implicit warning to all those who thrive on pranks, trickery and irreverence, suggesting that there will come a day when their mischievous nature catches up with them with potentially dire consequences. But as always, there is more than one way of seeing a Native American myth. The other way is that the story defuses some of the anxiety humans have about death, showing that it is not necessarily the end to life, but part of a fluid arrangement and interaction between different states of being, and even with some possibilities for fun.

BECAUSE HE DID NOT BELIEVE THAT HE WAS DEAD, HE DID NOT SEE THE GHOST WORLD WITH THE EYES OF A DEAD MAN.

Far right: Blue Jay sits in a canoe with his skeletal brother-in-law, the boat floating on the dead lake in the underworld.

GHOSTS, SPIRITS AND THE DEAD 117

118 GHOSTS, SPIRITS AND THE DEAD

THE DOUBLE-FACED GHOST (CHEYENNE)

The Cheyenne myth of the Double-Faced Ghost illustrates how the spirits still have many of the needs and desires of the living. Double-Face, as his name suggested, was a ghost who had two faces looking in opposite directions. He was a large spirit with long arms and fast legs that made him a superb hunter. Yet Double-Face was lonely and craved a wife to be by his side.

One day, Double-Face observed a human family nearby and fell deeply in love with the daughter. He was desperate to marry her, but rightly sensed that there were some existential obstacles to their union. So he set out to prove that he would make an ideal husband by hunting and collecting the finest meats, which he left outside the family's tipi every morning; the family awoke to find the puzzling but welcome gifts.

For several days the father of the family tried in vain to catch sight of who was leaving the food for them. After this time

Far left: A Cheyenne chief and his daughter. The chief wears the classic Native American war bonnet, created mainly from eagle feathers.

Below: An artistic representation of the ghost dance, painted onto a taut canvas of animal hide, shows the full communal experience of the event.

HE TOLD DOUBLE-FACE THAT HE COULD MARRY THE GIRL AS LONG AS HE WON IN A GAME OF HIDE-THE-PLUM-PIT.

passed, he maintained a vigil through the night and just before daybreak he saw what to his eyes was a terrible apparition – a huge two-faced ghost depositing armfuls of meat outside the tipi. The father woke his family at once, trembling with fear, and told them what he had seen. He bid them to rise, pack up all their belongings and the tipi, and flee.

When Double-Faced Ghost returned to the family's site the next morning, he found it empty with signs that they had fled in haste. He soon found the tracks they had left, and using the speed of his giant legs he quickly caught up with them and confronted the family. He told the father that his generosity was on account of wanting to marry his daughter. The father was fearful of raising the giant ghost's anger, so he suggested a way out of the situation. He told Double-Face that he could marry the girl as long as he won in a game of hide-the-plum-pit, telling the ghost that this was an essential tribal ritual to assess the suitability of a union. If he won he could marry the daughter, but if he lost he must go on his way.

The good-natured ghost consented, little knowing that the father was a true expert at this game and was rarely beaten. Furthermore, as the game was played the girl did her best to distract Double-Face with songs and conversation. Unable to focus and outplayed at every turn, Double-Face lost the game and his bride-to-be. Nevertheless, he kept on bringing the family meat because he was a kind and dutiful ghost.

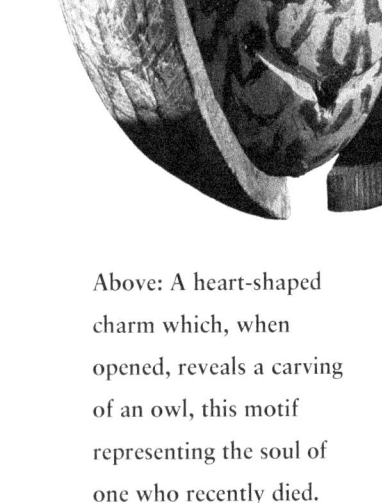

Above: A heart-shaped charm which, when opened, reveals a carving of an owl, this motif representing the soul of one who recently died.

THE ELK-CHARMER (SIOUX)

Of all the forces that appear to fracture the dividing lines between the dead and the living, it is love that is the most powerful and most common. Love, when fully embraced, is a state of passion that to those gripped by it seems to transcend the boundaries of time and existence. Such is evident in the Sioux myth of the ghostly Elk-Charmer, but with an interesting twist – those who abuse love and its power will reap a dark reward.

In ancient times, there lived a man who was highly desirable to women. He was young and handsome, but he also had the power to charm elk through playing magical music upon his flute. A by-product of this music was that women were also drawn to him, sometimes against their best intentions or attempts to resist where their feet were taking them. The tragedy of the situation was that the man had no interest in falling in love with the women who came to him; he just wanted to dominate them. For this reason, few people liked him.

One day, while out on a buffalo hunt, the man disappeared and did not return home to his village. His parents were anxious and went to the local medicine man for help. Using his 'finding stones', the medicine man told them that their son was in fact dead, for reasons that were unclear. Yet the medicine man was able to tell them the location of his body, so they went to the spot on the prairie and found him dead from a stab wound to the heart. The murderer was not found.

After undertaking the appropriate rites and preparations, the parents saw that the body of their son was placed high up on a funeral scaffold. Such was the evil of this act that the tribe left the territory to break the curse of what was likely to have been an internal act of violence.

Time passed and the people moved on from the terrible events of that day. Yet one evening, seemingly without reason, all the dogs in the camp started howling mournfully. Then the coyotes in the surrounding hills also joined this unsettling racket. Eventually

Above: The Elk-Charmer plays his magical music, and the women of the village are drawn impulsively towards the seductive tunes and the handsome man.

Above: A Zuni burial ceremony in New Mexico in the 1800s. The Hopi, Zuni and Pueblo peoples adopted burials earlier than many other Native American tribes, following their contact with the Spanish.

the howling stopped, but it was replaced by the hooting of the owls that signified death and the presence of ghostly spirits. The people took to their tipis, closing the flaps tightly against the coming darkness of the night.

It was then that they heard the noise, floating on the night air – the sound of the seductive elk flute. On top of this, they also heard a human voice, distantly familiar, that sang the following words:

> *Weeping I journey,*
> *Thinking it was just I*
> *Who had known the love of women.*
> *So many girls, so many women,*
> *Too many.*
> *But now I am in sorrow,*
> *Eternally roaming, never finding,*
> *This being my destiny*
> *For all time.*

THE FUNERAL SCAFFOLD

THE RITUALS FOR THE disposal of the dead varied from tribe to tribe in Native American culture. Some would bury their dead in a grave, a practice that became increasingly common with the spreading domination of white Christian culture during the 19th century and its attempts to stamp out what it saw as 'heathen' practices. A more traditional way of handling the body after it had been wrapped and prepared was to place it up in a tree or atop a funeral scaffold. The physical construction of such a scaffold was recorded by Dr H.C. Yarrow in his *Introduction to the Study of Mortuary Customs Among the North American Indians* (1880), who witnessed the scaffolds personally: 'These scaffolds are 7 to 8 feet high, 10 feet long, and 4 or 5 wide. Four stout posts, with forked ends, are first set firmly in the ground, and then in the forks are laid cross and side poles, on which is made a flooring of small poles. The body is then carefully wrapped, so as to make it watertight, and laid to rest on the poles. The reason why Indians bury in the open air instead of under the ground is for the purpose of protecting their dead from wild animals. In new countries, where wolves and bears are numerous, a dead body will be dug up and devoured, though it be put many feet under the ground. I noticed many little buckets and baskets hanging on the scaffolds... These had contained food and drink for the dead.'

Right: A funeral scaffold, elevated to keep the body away from ground-dwelling scavengers. Food would often be placed on the scaffold to sustain the deceased.

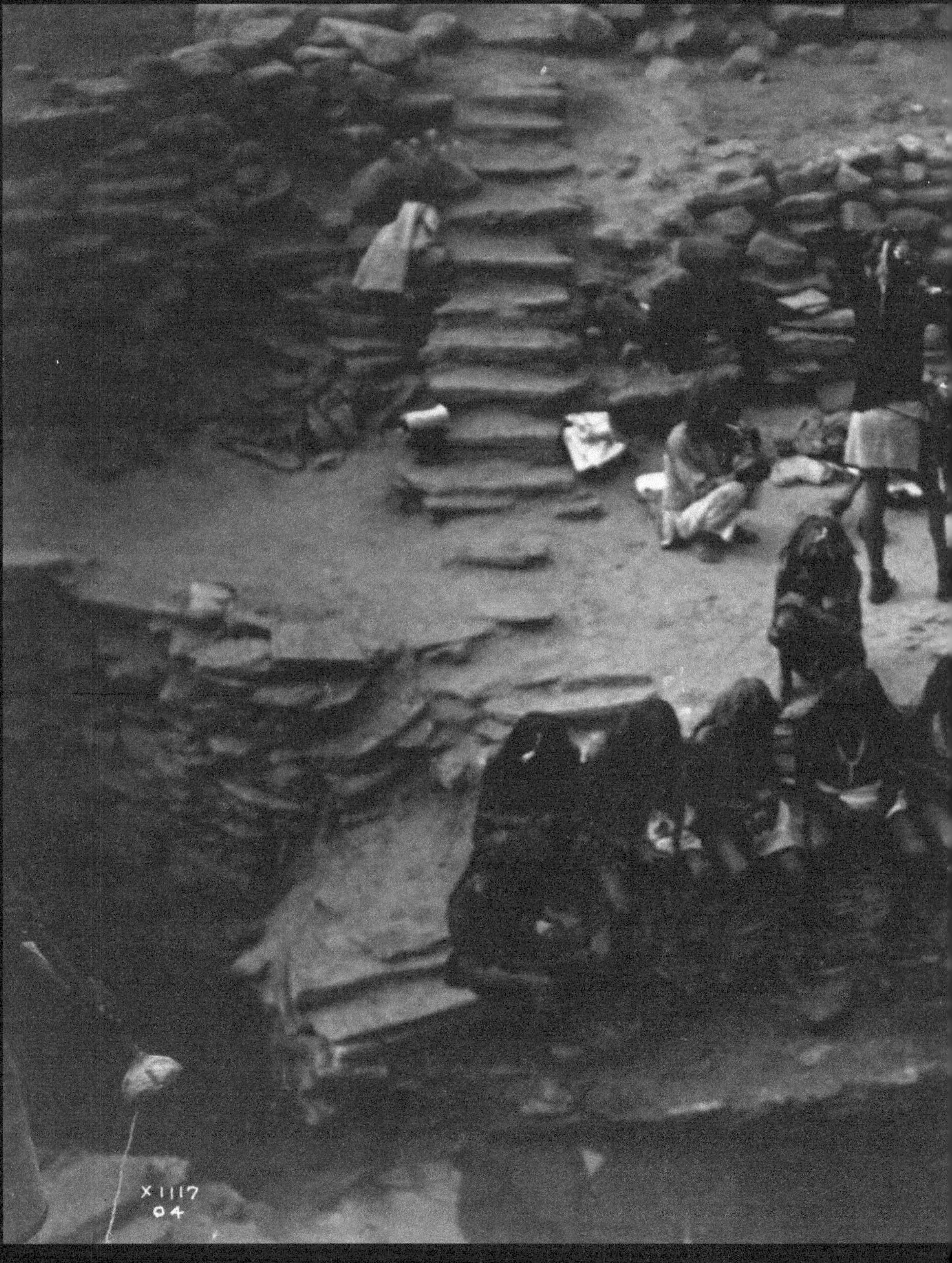
X1117
04

GHOSTS, SPIRITS AND THE DEAD   125

Left: A rare photograph of Native American flute dancers. The principal instruments of the traditional Native American tribes were percussion – such as drums and rattles – fiddles, and the two-chamber flute.

It was the ghostly voice of the Elk-Charmer, now saddened by death and longing. The spirit returned night after night, the music even drawing some women out into the darkness where they would see a spectral grey figure – the Elk-Charmer wrapped in his burial blanket – floating above the ground, forever consigned to drawing women to him but never knowing their embrace again.

This rather chilling tale gives a self-evident warning to over-amorous young men, cautioning that licentious behaviour will eventually produce potentially eternal consequences.

THE SKELETON HOUSE (HOPI)

Humanity is confronted by the fact of its own demise, a fundamental impulse that underpins all of the myths in this chapter and indeed many in this book. On occasions, we are drawn to reflect on this ending in a focused way, as is seen in the case of one young man in the Hopi myth of the Skeleton House, in which he directly experiences the spirit existence of the afterlife.

Below: Hopi children huddle together to talk and play. They wear cool, loose clothing, ideal for the daytime heat of the Arizona sun.

In the village of Shungopavi there lived a young man, son of the chief, who found himself constantly drawn to thinking about the experience of death and what came after. He would stare constantly at the graves around the village, lost in contemplation. He would also seek out elders and medicine men for answers, but even the wisest men seemed unable to give him the definitive information he was looking for.

Yet there was one individual – Badger Old Man – who could help with the young man's obsession, so the man's father sought him out. Badger Old Man was reputed to have special medicine that could reveal the secrets of what lay beyond the grave, so the father implored him to come and show these to his son. Badger Old Man agreed to help.

The next day, Badger Old Man gave special instructions to the villagers, for he needed their assistance to prepare the young man for his spiritual journey. Following his guidance closely, they dressed the young man exactly as they would if they were preparing the body of the deceased for burial: wearing a white kilt, with black paint on the chin and an eagle feather tied to his forehead. The young man, eager at last to know the truth about death – although still a little nervous about what was happening – surrendered himself to the ritual. Once he had been dressed and decorated as required, the young man lay down and Badger Old Man gave him some medicine to eat, also putting small quantities in his ears. After this, he wrapped the young man in a robe and waited.

> BADGER OLD MAN WAS REPUTED TO HAVE SPECIAL MEDICINE THAT COULD REVEAL THE SECRETS OF WHAT LAY BEYOND THE GRAVE.

Soon the medicine took effect and the young man 'died', falling into a deep and unnatural sleep that took him into the land of spirits. As he opened his eyes in the afterlife, he saw a long path leading towards the west. The destination, which he knew in advance, was the Skeleton House.

So the young man set out along the path. By the side of the road a short distance ahead sat a woman huddled near a ramshackle hut improvised out of sticks. 'Why are you here?' asked the woman. 'I'm here to discover the truth about death and the afterlife. Why are you here?' The woman looked thoughtful: 'I didn't follow the straight path, so I have to wait here many days before I can continue onwards to the Skeleton House.' Noting what she had said, the young man continued along the path.

He now came to a difficult part of his journey where the land was thick with tall and wide cacti, but he pushed through and eventually came to a steep cliff. There, near the edge, sat Kwaniita, a wise chief who wore an animal horn on his head and had a white line painted around his right eye. Kwaniita questioned the young man about his purpose, and when he told him Kwaniita pointed to the distance and said, 'Over there is the house that you are looking for.' But the young man could not see his goal on account of smoke swirling through the air. Kwaniita, however, showed him the way in the most dramatic fashion. He took off the man's kilt, lay it on the ground and then made the man sit on it. Suddenly Kwaniita flung the kilt into the air, and the garment carried the young man into the sky then gently floated down to deposit him at the bottom of the cliff. So he put on his kilt again and resumed his journey along the path.

> KWANIITA FLUNG THE KILT INTO THE AIR, AND THE GARMENT CARRIED THE YOUNG MAN INTO THE SKY THEN FLOATED DOWN TO DEPOSIT HIM AT THE BOTTOM OF THE CLIFF.

The next character the young man came across was Skeleton Woman, and he asked her about the origin of the smoke that stung his eyes and blurred his vision. She told him that the smoke came from the fire into which the wicked people of the village had been thrown, destruction being their punishment. The fire pit lay over one side of the track, and she cautioned the young man to stay firmly on the path.

Finally, the young man arrived at the Skeleton House. At first he saw few people – all skeletons – mainly children playing, but eventually others came to gather around him. Some of them remarked upon looking at him, 'A skeleton has come!'

Eventually they asked who he was, and he said 'I am the village chief's son, from the village of Shungopavi.' Responding, the villagers pointed towards the Bear Clan, saying that they were the young man's ancestors. He was taken to the Bear Clan lodge where he found that he was too heavy to climb the light ladder up to it, so he had to sit below while the skeletons brought him food.

Eventually the young man told the skeletons why he had come, and that he wanted to discover how they lived. They replied soberly: 'Life here is hard, with little to eat. Furthermore, we cannot eat food itself, only the odour of the food. The light here is also poor, and not as strong as in your world.' The young man looked around, satisfying his long-standing curiosity. He saw some of the dead staggering around carrying huge healing stones or bristling cacti on their backs as punishments for sins in life – they had to carry their burdens for a long period of time before they were finally relieved and forgiven. For those chiefs who had been good, they sat around their ceremonial fires wearing their *tiponis* (a Hopi badge of authority, usually consisting of an ear of corn decorated with feathers or a precious gem), the smoke from their fires wafting up into the world of the living, where it formed clouds.

Below: A vibrant rock painting of Kwataka, aka Man-eagle or Hopi Harpy, seen in the Desert View Watchtower, Grand Canyon National Park.

The dead spoke again to the young man. 'We must help each other. When you go back, make *nakwakwosis* for us at the Soyal ceremony. In return we will send you rain and good harvests.' (The *nakwakwosis* is a ceremonial talisman consisting of eagle or hawk feathers tied in a bundle.) They also gave the young man instructions on how to prepare the dead correctly to assist them in sending rainfall for the crops.

Eventually the young man knew he had seen and heard

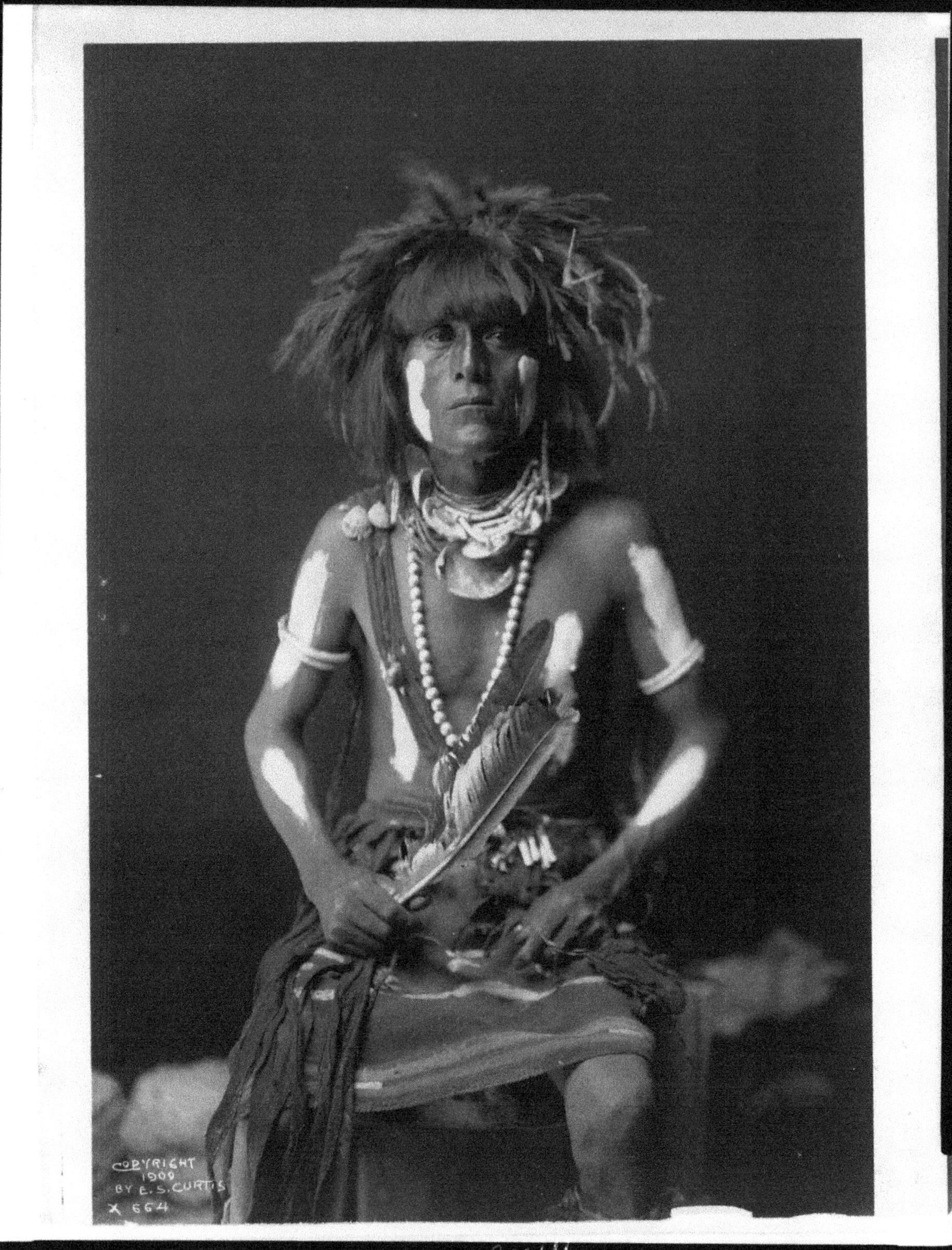
COPYRIGHT
1900
BY E.S. CURTIS
X 664

enough, and that he needed to go. He said his goodbyes and set off back down the track. When he reached the bottom of the steep cliff, he again stood on his kilt, which now lifted him back up to the top. Kwaniita was still there, and told him that his parents were mourning for him and that he needed to hasten home. Eventually he reached his house, at which point he broke the magic and his 'body' stirred from its mortal slumber aided by Badger Old Man.

Once he had awoken, eaten and was fully restored, he told the villagers of all he had discovered. He spoke of the hard life of the dead, noting that 'Here we are living in the light, but there they live in the dark. No one should ever desire to go there.' Yet he also explained his agreement with the dead, saying that in return for making prayer offerings to them, they in turn would send rain and crops. And thus it was that the dead and the living began to work for one another.

The myth of the Skeleton House is another example, quite literally, of the negotiation between the living and the dead in Native American mythology. It also contains a very clear thread of moral consequence, with evil deeds receiving punishment and good deeds receiving reward. Yet the myth also makes it clear that life in this world is preferable to that in the other. Ultimately, the myth implies that we must always embrace the physical life that we have, and avoid (albeit temporarily) the darkness to come.

Far left: A Hopi snake priest, clutching ceremonial eagle feathers. The snake priests would guide the village through the biannual snake dance ceremony.

Below: A Hopi corn festival – two women grind corn using *manos* and *metates*, while behind them three men maintain a rhythm on drums.

SPIRIT CREATURES

SOME NATIVE AMERICAN MYTHS have notions of specific races of spirits living among the natural world. These races have their own societies, but their world and that of the humans often collide, with the need for careful respect on both sides. One of the most endearing and detailed accounts of such a spirit race is that of the *Yunwi Tsunsdi*, or "Little People" of the Cherokee, as recorded here with some evident affection by James Mooney from the narratives of Cherokee elders:

'There is another race of spirits, the *Yunwi Tsunsdi*, or "Little People," who live in rock eaves on the mountain side. They are little fellows, hardly reaching up to a man's knee, but well shaped and handsome, with long hair falling almost to the ground. They are great wonder workers and are very fond of music, spending half their time drumming and dancing. They are helpful and kind-hearted, and often when people have been lost in the mountains, especially children who have strayed away from their parents, the *Yunwi Tsunsdi* have found them and taken care of them and brought them back to their homes. Sometimes their drum is heard in lonely places in the mountains, but it is not safe to follow it, because the Little People do not like to be disturbed at home, and they throw a spell over the stranger so that he is bewildered and loses his way, and even if he does at last get back to the settlement he is like one dazed ever after.

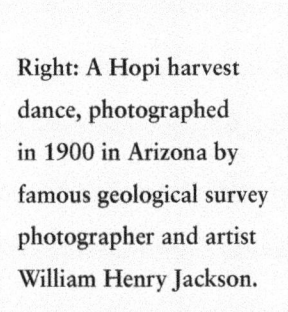

Right: A Hopi harvest dance, photographed in 1900 in Arizona by famous geological survey photographer and artist William Henry Jackson.

Left: A tree burial of the Oglala Sioux near Fort Laramie, Wyoming, the body stretched out on a scaffold between the branches.

Sometimes, also, they come near a house at night and the people inside hear them talking, but they must not go out, and in the morning they find the corn gathered or the field cleared as if a whole force of men had been at work. If anyone should go out to watch, he would die. When a hunter finds anything in the woods, such as a knife or a trinket, he must say, 'Little People, I want to take this,' because it may belong to them, and if he does not ask their permission they will throw stones at him as he goes home.

Once a hunter in winter found tracks in the snow like the tracks of little children. He wondered how they could have come there and followed them until they led him to a cave, which was full of Little People, young and old, men, women, and children. They brought him in and were kind to him, and he was with them some time; but when he left they warned him that he must not tell or he would die. He went back to the settlement and his friends were all anxious to know where he had been. For a long time he refused to say, until at last he could not hold out any longer, but told the story, and in a few days he died. Only a few years ago two hunters from Raventown, going behind the high fall near the head of Oconaluftee on the East Cherokee reservation, found there a cave with fresh footprints of the Little People all over the floor.'

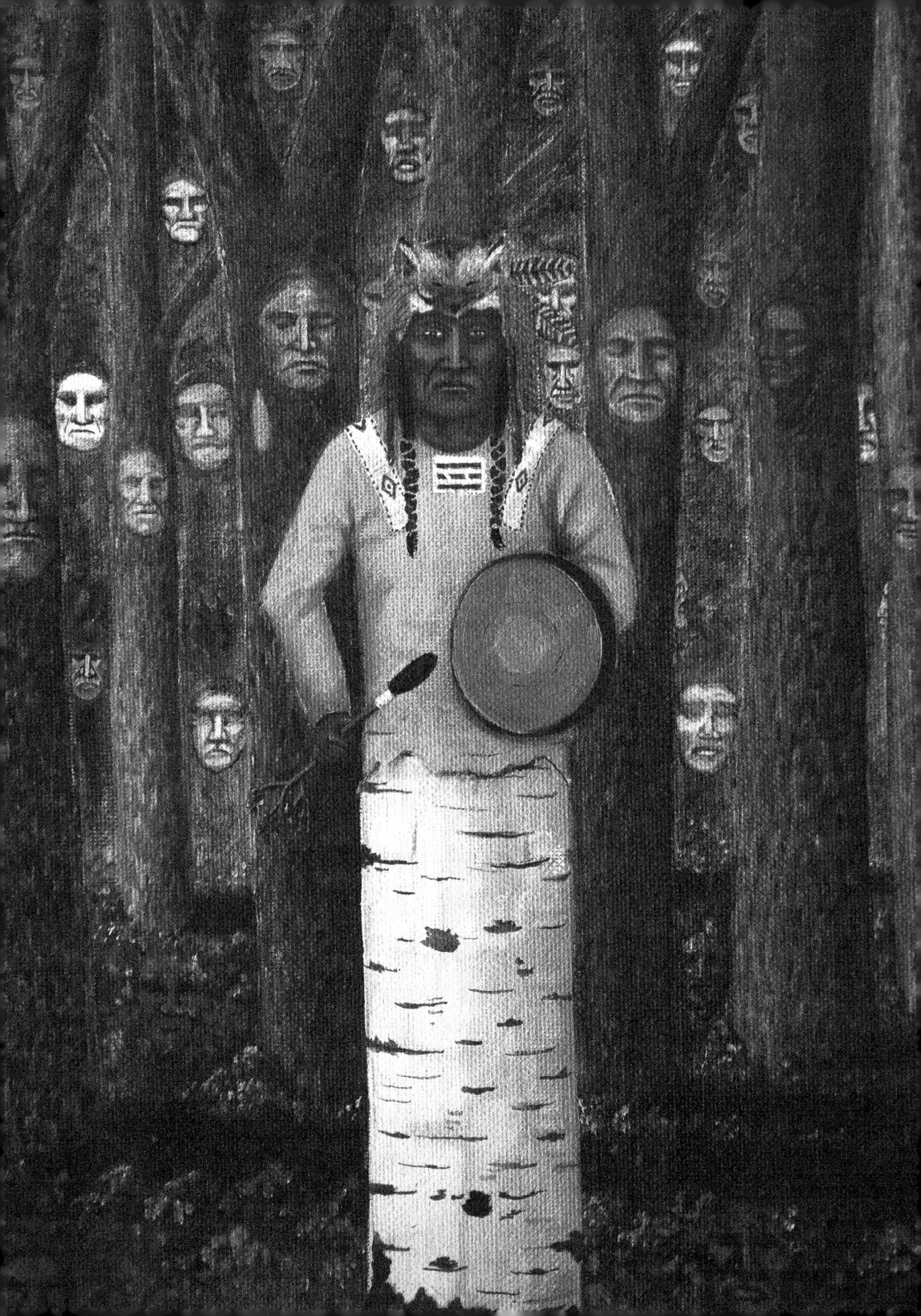

5

GODS, MONSTERS AND GREAT BEINGS

The range of characters in Native American legends and mythology is dizzying in its scope. Every possible permutation of nature and being is represented, from diminutive insects through to gods of creation.

THIS CHAPTER, however, will gravitate more towards the latter end of the scale, exploring some of the great figures – divine rulers, fearsome monsters and cultural heroes – that tower over tribal lore and identity. As we shall see, restricting our focus does nothing to lessen the diversity of the characters we encounter. In Native American mythology we can meet with gods disguised as people, gods in the form of animals, gods who are wise and kind, gods who are mercurial and violent, monsters who control the weather, monsters who bring order, monsters who cause chaos and evil, and divine creatures who give a moral compass to the world. We start, however, with one of the most compelling types of divine myth, in which human beings don't fully recognize the god within their midst.

Left: *Spirits of the Forest*, a painting by Jerome Kleine, perfectly captures the way that for Native American culture every aspect of the landscape is imbued with spirits and ancestral forces.

Right: A Navajo sand painting. Sand painting was used in various ceremonies, and in Navajo art the pigments mainly came from crushed sandstone of various colours, plus charcoal and plant materials.

THE SKY SPIRIT (NORTHWEST PACIFIC COAST)

One day, the daughter of a tribal chief was meandering along the seashore when she heard the sound of a baby crying. Disturbed, the girl hunted quickly for the source and found it to be from within a cockleshell. Opening it, she found a perfect dark-haired baby boy looking back up at her and smiling. Straight away she took the baby home, fearing that it had been abandoned, and began to raise him as her own child. Over time she married, and together the boy, young woman and her husband created a rounded and happy family, living out their life on the seashore.

The infant boy grew up healthy and bright, showing an interest in games and, above all, archery. His hands seemed to want to clasp a bow, so the woman made him one by hammering out one of her bracelets, complete with a set of needle-like arrows. With this set, the boy practised archery constantly and was quickly bringing down small prey such as rabbits and pigeons. It was clear that he was going to be a capable hunter, a fact that filled his parents with great pride.

One day, the boy's father decided to go out on a fishing trip and opted to take the boy with him. He was curious whether the skills the boy had shown hunting on land would be matched by skills in fishing from the sea. Yet at this time the boy was still too small to take out onto the water in the canoe, which often bucked and rocked on the waves, so the father decided to leave him on shore, from where he could initially observe the activities of fishing from a safe place. This the boy did with an almost unnatural intensity. Indeed, the father could almost have sworn that while the boy was staring at his boat, the sea around him became calmer and the weather above more hospitable.

Over time, the boy grew older, stronger and taller, eventually reaching sufficient stature to be able to accompany his father on the fishing trips. So one day the pair climbed into the canoe and together they sailed out to a fishing ground known for its favourable catches. The father made the first cast and almost instantly the line went taut. The boat was dragged across the sea at great speed, impelled

Left: A Sioux Native American raises his hand to the sky to invoke the power of the spirits.

Above: A peaceful scene of two Indian men river fishing, one man powering the boat gently, being careful not to startle the fish, while the other prepares to strike with a fish spear.

by a powerful force beneath the waves. Eventually, when the line finally relaxed, the father reeled in a truly enormous halibut, far bigger than any he had caught before. It had clearly been a fortuitous day.

But this was only the beginning. As long as the boy was with him, the hauls were perfect. It was as if the boy was his father's own personal good-luck charm. Then the day came when the boy – actually now a young man – disappeared. His parents were both distraught and puzzled, and could not fathom where he had gone. They searched everywhere for him, on land and at sea, but he seemed to have vanished without a trace. Yet then they glanced up into the sky, and were stunned by what they saw. Gliding gracefully over the ocean in the manner of a majestic bird, his arms outstretched and wreathed in cloud, was their son. He was wearing a cloak of feathers, those of the wren bird. And this was just the start. For the next two days he soared over the ocean in godlike fashion, one time wearing a cloak of jay feathers, the next day a cloak of woodpecker feathers. On each of the three flights, the sea beneath him changed in its nature.

On the first day it was cold, grey and flat; on the next day it glowed with silver and gold sheens; on the third day it looked as if the sea itself were afire.

With these demonstrations of aerial greatness, the young man established that he was none other than the Spirit of the Sky, the great celestial deity. Eventually, the Spirit of the Sky descended back down to the ground to visit his earthly parents. Although he had now taken his rightful place in the heavens, he still felt love for them. To his father he said, 'When you plan to go fishing, look up to the heavens, for if there you shall see my face, you will know that it is a safe and auspicious day to go fishing, and your catch will be great.' Then to his mother, the woman who had rescued him from the seashore all those years ago, he said, 'Mother, I will never forgot all the kindness and devotion that you have shown to me. Thus I will give you the gift of the ability to control the weather.' With that he gave her a magical cloak. When she put it on, but opened it out wide with her arms, the weather became tempestuous and stormy, with rain lashing and wind pummelling the land and sea. But when she closed the cloak tightly back around her body, all the storms were pulled back in and the weather grew calm once more. From that time forward, she became the Fine Weather Woman, able to control the very climate itself. Sometimes, when her son, the Spirit of the Sky, was angry and caused storms to flash across the heavens, she would calm his temper by throwing a ball of feathers up into the air. These would gently float back down to the Earth again as snow, and all would become calm.

> WITH THESE DEMONSTRATIONS OF AERIAL GREATNESS, THE YOUNG MAN ESTABLISHED THAT HE WAS THE SPIRIT OF THE SKY, THE GREAT CELESTIAL DEITY.

Below: A Native American charm mask. The face on this mask represents the spirit of the Moon, the board around the face symbolizes air, the hoops the levels of the cosmos, and the feathers act as stars in the heavens.

The myth of the Spirit of the Sky and the Fine Weather Woman bring the human and divine into a direct and consequential relationship. The more that the humans care for the gods, the more they return the favour, until heaven and Earth achieve a perfect balance and cooperation. The myth also tells us that the divine may reside where we do not expect it, even in our children, hence it encourages a devout and circumspect attitude.

THE THUNDERBIRD (SIOUX)

The story of the Spirit of the Sky makes a firm connection between the weather and the presence, even the emotions, of the divine. This is a classic association, and an understandable one – the Native American tribes, particularly when still living a traditional natural lifestyle, would have sought heavenly explanations for the awesome power of nature, from tornadoes and great storms through to endless days of summer heat and sparkling spring rains.

One of the most pervasive of the weather gods, encountered in various myths occurring across North America, is that of the Thunderbirds. The origins and presentation of Thunderbirds varies according to the source and structure of the myth, but the common image is of a huge heavenly bird, typically eagle-like in nature, whose awesome wings bring thunder as they fracture the heavens, while lightning bolts shoot from their burning eyes.

Although the Thunderbird is especially associated with the Native American cultures of the Pacific Northeast, it is also encountered among people such as the Algonquian, Winnebago and Sioux. Among the latter, it is known as *Wakinyan Tanka*, or the Great Thunderbird.

Below: A depiction of the great Thunderbird, a figure of terrible power – controller of the heavenly elements and bringer of thunder and lightning – but also one that could be the protector of humans.

Traditional Sioux mythology has four Thunderbirds, one for each point of the compass, each with different physical characteristics and colouration, but all terrifying to behold. Yet few humans have seen these apparitions, for when they fly they are wrapped in vast expanses of black cloud from which bolts of flaming lightning run down to the ground. And yet, for all of their mighty and numinous appearance, they were actually not ill disposed to the human race as long as the humans practised truth and honesty in their dealings with one another and with the spirits. In fact, the Thunderbirds would even rise to the defence of the humans, as the myth of the Thunderbirds and the Unktehi demonstrates.

The Great Unktehi, greatest of all the Unktehi, was a dreadful and destructive water monster, the largest of a whole race of such aquatic beasts. Great Unktehi was known for her contempt of human beings, and for generating floods, causing even the mighty Mississippi River to burst its banks and kill thousands of people on either side.

The Thunderbirds observed this behaviour bitterly from the heavens, their great spirits moved to pity and protection for the helpless humans. *Wakinyan Tanka*, in anger, declared that the Thunderbirds must rise against the Unktehi creatures. So it was that a battle of the gods and monsters took place. Even though the Thunderbirds were well equipped for the fight, with their fearsome claws and beaks, the water monsters were brutally powerful, with muscular bodies, cruel mouths and spiked tails.

In the first phase of the war, the Thunderbirds found themselves fighting a losing battle. They flew down to attack the water monsters on land and in the water itself, environments that favoured the fighting style

Left: The Thunderbird as shown on a Pawnee ceremonial drum. It was an important creature, for its control of the elements meant that it was also responsible for the watering of crops.

Below: This carved wooden figure from the Tsimshian people of Canada shows the Thunderbird, with its warlike visage.

142 GODS, MONSTERS AND GREAT BEINGS

Standing on the bow of this canoe, a masked man impersonates the Thunderbird during a wedding ceremony, dancing as others row to the nearby shore of the bride's village.

ALL THE THUNDERBIRDS GATHERED TOGETHER IN THE DARK AND ROLLING CLOUDS, AND AT THE VERY SAME INSTANT SENT OUT THEIR LIGHTNING BOLTS.

of Unktehi and her kin. So the Thunderbirds retreated to a high mountain where they held a war council. *Wakinyan Tanka* declared that they should not fight on the ground, but instead should use their powers to control and create the weather. So all the Thunderbirds gathered together in the dark and rolling clouds, and at the very same instant sent out their lightning bolts into the waters below. The incredible heat instantly boiled the rivers dry, killing the Unktehi as they lost the water in which they swam. Only their bones were left, bleached and crumbling in the sun. Thus it was that the Thunderbirds defeated the Unktehi, and the human survivors below offered up prayers of gratitude forever.

CREATURES OF TERROR

While the Thunderbirds strike us with awe, akin to that of encountering a god, there are a lesser collection of Native American monsters that generate a more primal terror, creatures that inhabit the darkest corners of both nature and the human psyche. These monsters have a variety of forms, but lean towards hybridity, mixing the most insidious traits of one species with those of another. A case in point is the Water Panther, also known as *Mishipeshu* or *Mishibijiw*, who stalks the waterways of the northeastern woodlands and lakes.

Below: A Tlingit shaman's rattle crafted into the form of a great sea monster. On the monster's back, the shaman tortures a witch figure.

The Water Panther (Anishinaabe)

The Water Panther (alternatively 'Water Lynx') is particularly common among the Anishinaabe grouping of Native American people and the Ojibwe, Ojibwa or Chippewa. Descriptions of the creature vary somewhat from place to place. Certainly the main part of its physique is that of a large wild cat, but some descriptions have its body covered in scales, with spikes running down the length of its spine. Furthermore, unlike the standard land-dwelling cat, the Water Panther is – as its name suggests – an aquatic monster, living in deep lakes and rivers, swimming silently to the surface to prey on those who stray too near or causing storms and whirlpools. Such was its power that some tribes regard it literally as an underworld god.

A Wisconsin Chippewa tale of the Water Panther, collected by Victor Barnouw in the 1970s, illustrates the unnerving nature of the creature. As the legend goes, one tribal land was wrapped around a large lake, and in the lake was a muddy, stinking island, laced through with waterways. The island sat square in the middle of the lake and anyone rowing across had to deviate around it, giving it a wide berth on account of its status as cursed place. On one particular occasion, a village on one side of the lake was holding a celebration, and those on the other side were invited. Most of the guests from the other side of the lake set off rowing in plenty of time, going around the island as caution dictated.

However, two women who were sisters-in-law were running late. The one who was rowing decided that to save time, she would go straight through the mud-island, much to the alarm of her companion. As the boat was inching its way uneasily through the muddy channels, they came to an open patch of clear water and rowed into it. Although the water was clear, it was swirling and bubbling in an unnatural way.

All of a sudden, an angry Water Panther emerged from the depths, whipping the boat with its tail to try to turn it over to get at the women within. The sister-in-law who had not been rowing carried with her a small cedar oar for ceremonial and decorative purposes. With quick wits, she hacked down on the panther's tail as it whipped over the edge of the boat, chopping the tip off and shouting out, 'Thunder is striking you!' as she attacked.

Above: A rock painting of Mishipeshu, the Water Panther, showing its spiked back and long, whipping tail, the latter bringing river floods and sinking boats.

146   GODS, MONSTERS AND GREAT BEINGS

Below: Carved by Wabanaki artisans in Quebec, Canada, this image forms part of a bas relief entitled 'Life Path', showing Wabanaki traditions and words of wisdom.

The Water Panther squealed and ran away through the mud. When the women picked up the portion of tail that lay inside the boat, they found that it was made of pure copper. One of the women eventually gave the piece of tail to her father, and whenever he took it with him hunting or fishing it always brought luck.

Chenoo (Wabanaki)

Another Native American monster that brought fear to young and old alike when it was brought alive in campfire stories was the Chenoo, or the ice giant. Most prevalent among the people of the Wabanaki Confederacy in the northwestern United States and western Canada, but also found with other names along the forested Eastern Seaboard, the Chenoo were the embodiment of evil. The legend went that the Chenoo were originally human beings, but they committed such heinous crimes, or were possessed by such devilish spirits, that their hearts turned to ice. In this state, they become large man-eating cannibals, preying mercilessly on the unwary in the wilderness.

The possibility of being transformed into a Chenoo drew out a special fear in many tribes, much in the same way the werewolf caused psychological terror over parts of continental Europe during the medieval period. This chill threat is perfectly explained in this Algonquian myth from New England, recorded in the late 19th century. During one autumn time, 10 families sailed up the Saguenay River and followed a branch of the river into a particularly icy and snowy part of the region. Among the travellers was a young woman of great beauty. One other member of the party, an amorous young man, was infatuated with the girl and asked for her hand in marriage, but she refused. The young man, immature as he was angry, decided to exact his revenge.

He went out into the forest around them and gathered a herb that induced a deep, unnaturally long sleep. He also collected a large ball of ice. Sneaking up on the girl one night, he wafted the herb under her nose and she slipped into unconsciousness. Then he placed the ball of ice just under her chin, upon her throat, and left it there. For many, many hours she slept, as the ice struck a

Above: The Saguenay River that flows through Quebec is known for its fast-flowing waters and its dangerous flooding.

something grumpy and hostile. It was also clear that she was ill, having a deep burning sensation inside her. The only thing that could ease the burn was eating snow, which she began to do voraciously. The changes, however, grew steadily more sinister. Eventually she began to manifest murderous and evil tendencies, even to those she loved. Yet she possessed just enough self-awareness to know what was happening – she was being transformed into a Chenoo. Knowing that death was the only release from the transformation, the girl told her parents that they had to kill her, or she would kill them. 'How do we kill you?', asked the mother. 'You must shoot me with seven arrows, and if you cannot kill me with seven arrows then there is the danger that I will destroy you all.' So seven warriors gathered around her as she sat on the floor looking calm and unafraid. They shot her accurately with seven arrows, but she scarcely flinched, simply staring at the men with an unsettling smile. On the warriors went, shooting her continually and frantically, aiming for the heart every time. Eventually, after the 49th arrow had pierced her body, she keeled over dead.

With urgency, the men now cut the body into tiny pieces and threw them on the fire, burning them into ash. The frozen, icy heart, however, took much work to melt and destroy, but eventually even this too was gone. Yet such was the terror of the Chenoo that the tribe left that land for good, terrified that one small piece of the body might have been left and this alone would regenerate into a Chenoo.

Wendigo (Algonquian)
While the Chenoo is little known outside the Native American community and those interested in its lore, the same cannot be said of the Wendigo, also known as the Windigo, which has become a popular figure in Western comic books and supernatural TV shows. The grotesque figure of the Wendigo appears in the mythologies of the forested and Great Lakes regions of both the northern United States and Canada. The

> WHEREVER THE WENDIGO PROWLED, IT SEEMED AS IF FROZEN WEATHER AND FAMINE WOULD MOVE WITH HIM.

descriptions of the nature and the appearance of the creature shift according to local traditions, but they are invariably terrifying and malevolent. Typically the Wendigo has the appearance of a gaunt, skeletal but supernaturally strong human, but with an insatiable appetite for human flesh and blood. It was a cannibalistic being with hideous burning eyes, rotting skin and a foul, dead smell – in many ways, the Wendigo looked for all intents and purposes like a demonic reanimated corpse that stalked the woodlands and villages at night, looking for the vulnerable to snatch and consume. Wherever he prowled, it seemed as if frozen weather and famine would move with him. In some myths he was also a giant, growing in size and power with every human he ate.

There are numerous local legends about moments when humans were confronted with the Wendigo. One of these, another recording of the late 19th century around the Great Lakes, reflects a very deep-seated fear among the people that the Wendigo could possess their most treasured possession: their children. In this legend, a child was born to a young couple who doted on their new baby. One day, when the child should still have been too young to talk, he said a strange thing: 'Where is that *manidogisik* [Sky Spirit]? All say he is very powerful and one day I am going to visit him'. This declaration seemed irreverent to the parents, who admonished the child for saying such a thing.

Below: The shadow of a Wendigo falls on the ground in a Carolinian forest. Wendigo legends still haunt the forests of the eastern United States to this day.

A few nights later, the parents were sleeping with the baby lying between them in a cot. Suddenly, the mother awoke with a start to find that the cot was empty. She woke her husband in a panic and they lit torches and began searching frantically. Eventually, outside their lodge, they found the tiny footprints of their child heading down towards the lake. They began following them, but as they went along the footprints steadily became larger and larger until they were far bigger than those of a natural human. With an agonizing horror, the parents realized that their baby was being transformed into a Wendigo. Furthermore, the Wendigo was heading out across the now-frozen lake, intent on confronting the *manidogisik*. Now the *manidogisik* saw the Wendigo approaching, and sent out his loyal army of supernatural little people to head off the threat; they had the power to throw rocks as if they were bolts of lightning. Eventually they hit the Wendigo with the lightning-rocks, and the ghastly creature – once a beautiful baby – fell down dead. As with the Chenoo, it was imperative that the body was utterly obliterated. This was not easy, because although he had an outward human appearance, inside he was just like a huge block of ice, which had to be hacked into little pieces. Eventually those destroying the body found the corpse of the tiny infant right in the centre.

Below: The Wendigo exerts a pull over modern TV and cinema. Here we see the creature as depicted in the popular TV series *Charmed*.

Nun'yunu'wi, The Stone Man (Cherokee)

Cannibalism is a thread of terror that appears intermittently in Native American myth. The

WENDIGO PSYCHOSIS

Since European settlers began to populate the United States in earnest from the 17th century, dark rumours circulated of Native American individuals who were transformed into the Wendigo, committing terrible cannibalistic acts. One horrifying account from French Jesuit missionaries, recorded in 1661, is given with a definite sense of journalistic reportage:

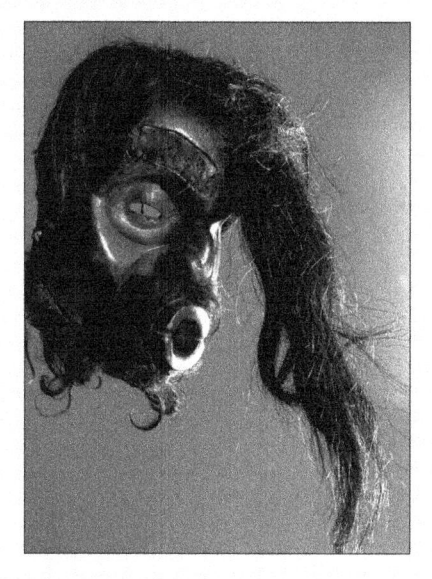

Left: A grotesque mask representing Tsonoqua – the wild woman of the woods – a giantess who carried away children in order to eat them.

'What caused us greater concern was the intelligence that met us upon entering the Lake, namely, that the men deputed by our Conductor for the purpose of summoning the Nations to the North Sea, and assigning them a rendezvous, where they were to await our coming, had met their death the previous Winter in a very strange manner. Those poor men (according to the report given us) were seized with an ailment unknown to us, but not very unusual among the people we were seeking. They are afflicted with neither lunacy, hypochondria nor frenzy; but have a combination of all these species of disease, which affects their imaginations and causes them a more than canine hunger. This makes them so ravenous for human flesh that they pounce upon women, children and even upon men, like veritable werewolves, and devour them voraciously, without being able to appease or glut their appetite – ever seeking fresh prey, and the more greedily the more they eat. This ailment attacked our deputies; and, as death is the sole remedy among those simple people for checking such acts of murder, they were slain in order to stay the course of their madness.'

Although it is easy to write such accounts off as fantasy, several other well-documented cases crop up during the 18th and 19th centuries, and even into the early 20th century. Psychologists have argued over the interpretation, but the label 'Wendigo Psychosis' has been applied, indicating a culturally specific form of madness that expresses itself by modelling the folkloric behaviours of the Wendigo.

act of eating another human appears more than just grotesque and barbaric; it is akin to spiritual possession, the consuming of a soul as much as a body. We have already seen several cannibalistic myths from the northern parts of North America, but the great James Mooney recorded – albeit with some of the biological puritanism common in the 19th century – another myth from among the Cherokee, and it is the story of Nun'yunu'wi, The Stone Man:

'Once when all the people of the settlement were out in the mountains on a great hunt one man who had gone on ahead climbed to the top of a high ridge and found a large river on the other side. While he was looking across he saw an old man walking about on the opposite ridge, with a cane that seemed to be made of some bright, shining rock. The hunter watched and saw that every little while the old man would point his cane in a certain direction, then draw it back and smell the end of it. At last he pointed it in the direction of the hunting camp on the other side of the mountain, and this time when he drew back the staff he sniffed it several times as if it smelled very good, and then started along the ridge straight

Below: Native American Nakoaktok dancers wear masks of the mythical Kotsuis birds during a traditional potlatch in 1914, in British Columbia, Canada. The costumes represent Kotsuis and Hohhuq, servants of the man-eating monster Pahpaqalanohsiwi.

Above: In the Cherokee legend of the Stone Man, the old man creates a rock bridge by throwing his magical cane into the air.

for the camp. He moved very slowly, with the help of the cane, until he reached the end of the ridge, when he threw the cane out into the air and it became a bridge of shining rock stretching across the river. After he had crossed over upon the bridge it became a cane again, and the old man picked it up and started over the mountain toward the camp.

'The hunter was frightened, and felt sure that it meant mischief, so he hurried on down the mountain and took the shortest trail back to the camp to get there before the old man. When he got there and told his story the medicine man said the old man was a wicked cannibal monster called Nun'yunu'wi, "Dressed in Stone," who lived in that part of the country and was always going about the mountains looking for some hunter to kill and eat. It was very hard to escape from him because his stick guided him like a dog, and it was nearly as hard to kill him, because his whole body was covered with a skin of solid rock. If he came he would kill and eat them all, and there was only one way to save themselves. He could not bear to look upon a menstrual woman, and if they could find seven menstrual women to stand in the path as he came along the sight would kill him.

Above: Marching to the rhythm of ceremonial rattles, a dance of the Jemez Pueblo, a community of people who still live in Sandoval County, New Mexico.

'So they asked among all the women, and found seven who were sick in that way, and with one of them it had just begun. By the order of the medicine man they stripped themselves and stood along the path where the old man would come. Soon they heard Nun'yunu'wi coming through the woods, feeling his way with his stone cane. He came along the trail to where the first woman was standing, and as soon as he saw her he started and cried out: "*Yu!* My grandchild; you are in a very bad state!" He hurried past her, but in a moment he met the next woman, and cried out again: "*Yu!* My child; you are in a terrible way," and hurried past her, but now he was vomiting blood. He hurried on and met the third and the fourth and the fifth woman, but with each one that he saw his step grew weaker until when he came to the last one, with whom the sickness had just begun, the blood poured from his mouth and he fell down on the trail.

'Then the medicine man drove seven sourwood stakes through his body and pinned him to the ground, and when night came they piled great logs over him and set fire to them, and all the people gathered around to see. Nun'yunu'wi was a great ada'wehi and knew many secrets, and now as the fire came close to him he began to talk, and told them the medicine for all kinds of sickness. At midnight he began to sing, and sang the hunting songs for calling up the bear and the deer and all the animals of the woods and mountains. As the blaze grew hotter his voice sank low and lower, until at last when daylight came the logs were a heap of white ash and the voice was still.

'Then the medicine man told them to rake off the ashes, and where the body had lain they found only a large lump of red wa'di paint and a magic u'lunsu'ti stone. He kept the stone for himself, and calling the people around him he painted them, on face and breast, with the red wa'di, and whatever each person prayed for while the painting was being done – whether for hunting success, for working skill or for a long life – that gift was his.'

> THEN THE MEDICINE MAN DROVE SEVEN SOURWOOD STAKES THROUGH HIS BODY AND PINNED HIM TO THE GROUND.

One interesting thread to emerge from many of these narratives is that a monster's body has to be obliterated completely for its killers to be reassured that it will not come back, hence destruction by fire is the preferred method of disposal. Yet so often there is something indestructible, or nearly so – a core element of the creature that remains and either requires far more work to destroy, or it actually becomes a talisman through which positive magic can be performed or which attracts good luck. In the latter cases, there is almost a message of redemption, that even when wrapped in evil there was an element that could still be classed as good.

PAMOLA (PENOBSCOT)

While many of the monsters recounted in this chapter are implacably unfriendly, Native American mythology often allows for even the most evil of creature to be fickle and flexible at times, and even to exhibit mercy. A classic example is a Penobscot tale concerning the evil spirit Pamola (or Pomola), meaning 'He curses on the mountain'. The exact nature of this creature is unclear – he was certainly a malign and gigantic bird, capable of swooping down and snatching up a fully grown human or large mammal – but some legends also have him sporting a moose's head. Either way, he lived upon Mount Katahdin in Maine, and from there not only preyed upon the humans of the land around him, but also summoned forth storms, snow, wind and spooky dark nights.

Yet there is a legend of a time when Pamola exhibited a degree of mercy. The story goes that, in times past, likely the 17th century, a hunter was encamped on the slopes of Mount Katahdin during an autumn hunt. Suddenly, a brutal blizzard descended and the snow piled up high around the hunter's camp,

Below: A graphic depiction of a Penobscot warrior hunting moose in the frozen forests, firing multiple arrows into this large prey animal to bring it down.

trapping him in his meagre makeshift hut. He did not have any snowshoes with him, and thus he remained where he was, unable to move and running out of food as the hours turned into days. Now he knew that high above him dwelt Pamola, who could control the elements, so he offered up a sacrifice of oil and fat to the god-monster, burning the substances over a coal fire. The scent of the sacrifice ascended to Pamola, who found it pleasing. The winged monster therefore took off from the summit and flew down to the camp to see who was there.

As Pamola landed at the camp he was met by the hunter, who said out loud: 'Welcome to you, partner.' Pamola stared at the plucky human with his fierce eyes, but then said: 'It is good that you have called me partner – if you had called me by any other name I would have killed you. You are the first and the only person who has ever called on me and lived, for I have devoured all the others. For this offering, I will take you up onto the mountain, and you shall live happily with me'.

So Pamola compelled the man to close his eyes and climb up onto the spirit bird's back. With that, Pamola took off with his majestic wings, flew up above the clouds and then down into the heart of the mountain. Once inside, the man was surprised by what he saw – a surprisingly domestic scene. Pamola lived with a human-like wife and children, housed in a spacious and well-kept tipi. There was a well-stocked larder, replete with all the fine meats and food Pamola had taken from Mount Katahdin and the surrounding landscape. Pamola spoke to the man with some kindness. 'You will live with us here for one year, in which time you shall not leave the mountain. I will give you my daughter as

Above: On a cliff of the Mississippi River near Alton, Illinois, a painting (a modern reproduction) depicts the legendary Piasa winged monster, an evil creature eventually killed with poisoned arrows.

a wife, and you will have all the food and luxuries you desire. After one year has passed, you are free to go down the mountain to see your own people, but you are free to return here and spend as much time with us as you like. There is only one condition – that you must never marry again. If you do, I will swoop down, gather you up and bring you back to the mountain, from where you will never be able to leave again.'

So it came to pass. The man took Pamola's daughter for his wife and lived well upon the mountain. A year later, he decided to visit his people once again, and while there he told them all that had occurred. The people fêted him and his stories, and he stayed with them for longer and longer without going back to Pamola's lair and his family in the mountain. The local people offered him their daughters for marriage, and at first the man refused, honouring the promise he had made to Pamola. But over time his will was eroded, and eventually he agreed to marry one particular local girl. When the day of the wedding came, however, the man was nowhere to be seen. All the locals now felt that Pamola, angered by the way the man had reneged on his agreement, had come down from the mountain and taken him back there, never to leave.

GLOOSKAP (WABANAKI)

The myth of Pamola and the hunter illustrates how even the most evil creature might, on occasion, be capable of demonstrating contrasting qualities. In addition, Native American mythology is also a landscape populated with heroic and noble beings, who through wisdom or humane action counterbalance the darkness that is interweaved through humanity. In fact, there are heroic figures who attain the status of what we now call 'culture heroes', those whose character represents almost a pillar of tribal identity.

Below: A collection of Native American artefacts from daily life. Such artefacts were also a form of currency among the tribes, having a tradeable value in themselves.

A prime example of such a figure is Glooskap (also Glooscap), again of the Wabanaki people. The myths and legends surrounding Glooskap are many and varied, so describing him precisely is difficult and resists easy summary. He certainly has a divine or semi-divine status. In the Abenaki tradition, for example, he was formed by the creator god Tabaldak, and was also given powers of creation over elements of the world. In the Penobscot traditions, Glooskap was the creator of human beings. Yet alongside this status as a being of divine power, he is also a cultural hero with a decidedly human side to his personality – he could be a trickster spirit, for example, playing morally significant pranks on people and animals, albeit never with cruelty or malice. In fact, Glooskap is decidedly a moral force for good, opposed to the dark forces of the world and intervening on humanity's behalf in ethical clashes. On occasions, however, his morality can be evidenced in a hardness of character, as is seen in the following Mi'kmaq myth, one of countless about this potent figure.

Glooskap lived on an island in the middle of a huge lake wreathed in mist, which was in fact the smoke that curled out from Glooskap's pipe. Knowing that he had the power to grant wishes to people, four men from a village decided to sail out to the island to meet with the great being and see if he would

Right: A Mi'kmaq canoe. Cedar wood was typically used to form the canoe's frame, with birchbark forming the outer waterproof covering.

grant them their dreams. The first man desperately wanted to be wealthy so he could experience the life of the rich. The second man wanted physical improvements – he wanted to be tall and powerfully built, in contrast to his short, slim frame, as he felt that being so would demand more respect from his fellow men. The third man was getting old and started to see death on the horizon – he wanted the gift of eternal life. The fourth individual, by contrast, simply wanted to be a capable hunter so that he could provide for his family more reliably and confidently.

So it was that the four men set out in a canoe for Glooskap's island. It was not to be an easy journey. At one point, a brutal wind whipped up, threatening to blow the boat off course or onto rocks. The first man, however, made an offering of tobacco, and the smoke from this calmed the wind. Then the sea became white-capped and stormy, and there was the danger that the canoe would be flooded and sink or that it would capsize. Now the second man stepped up to save the day, singing a gentle melody in such bewitching tones that even the sea became calm at the sound.

The next tribulation came from a huge whale, which leapt from the water next to the boat, crashing down and nearly overturning them. As it thrashed about with its tail smashing the water – and potentially the boat – the third man used a magic whalebone charm, settling the creature and sending it on its way by throwing the charm into the water. Finally, as they approached Glooskap's island, the fourth man used the smoke from a magic pipe to part the seemingly impenetrable mist around the island.

Eventually they reached their destination and made their way nervously and reverently until they stood before the great Glooskap. Having made their obeisance, they then spoke their wishes to him who considered them thoughtfully. After a period of silence, Glooskap spoke. 'I shall indeed grant you your wishes. They are contained in these four pouches,' – he handed each of them a small buckskin pouch, tied at the neck – 'but I warn you,

> NOW THE SECOND MAN STEPPED UP TO SAVE THE DAY, SINGING A GENTLE MELODY IN SUCH BEWITCHING TONES THAT EVEN THE SEA BECAME CALM AT THE SOUND.

Above: A statue of Glooskap at the Truro Heritage Centre, Nova Scotia. Glooskap has numerous myths attached to his name among the Wabanaki peoples, being a cultural hero.

you must not open these until you reach your homes'.

With that Glooskap sent them on their way, each man euphoric at the thought that their greatest desires were about to become realities. As they paddled back, however, curiosity began to niggle away at them. It was a long journey, after all, and what could be the harm of having a look in the pouches? So the first man, he who had desired riches, carefully opened the bag and peaked inside. As he did so, he unleashed an endless torrent of luxurious goods from within – fine clothes, hunting weapons, jewellery, tipis, games and ornaments – all came rushing out until the boat filled up and sank. The man who had wanted riches was dragged down to the bottom of the lake and drowned.

The other three men managed to swim to shore, clutching their bags tightly. Yet they still had to walk home, and curiosity continued to do its work. The second man, who wished to be tall, therefore opened the neck of his pouch. In an instant he began to get taller... and taller and taller. For the first few inches of growth he was excited, but then he ascended many, many feet up into the air. More alarmingly, his body was hardening and becoming wooden – he was turning into a tree! Eventually his growth stopped, but now he was a mighty tree, taller than all men but rooted to one spot for endless decades.

The third man also relented on his journey home, opening the bag against Glooskap's express warnings. As he did so, he felt his body becoming frozen, rigid and collapsing in on itself. Eventually his whole frame was turned into a rock, a large and impregnable stone that would exist for all eternity.

Of the men who made the trip to Glooskap, only the fourth man did as commanded. He reached his home and, once safely inside and alone, gently opened the bag that had been given to him. It was as if his senses came alive in the most extraordinary way. All of a sudden he could see and hear animals with incredible acuity. Furthermore, he could hear voices from all of them, as if giving him instructions on how to find and hunt them. With this newfound skill, the man was always able to provide for his family, who flourished in health and happiness.

The powerful narrative element of this myth is that Glooskap, although he only makes a physical appearance at the beginning of the story, actually feels present throughout the whole narrative, as if he was a huge all-seeing eye watching over events. The fact that the first three men wished for vain or selfish rewards seems to have almost guaranteed their fate, from the moment they first travelled to see Glooskap to the moment they opened their pouches. The undesirable nature of their wishes makes it feel inevitable that they would bring ill consequences upon themselves, and that Glooskap knew this would always be the case. Yet the man who had humble and selfless desires, and who obeyed Glooskap's commands, reaps the rewards.

In this tale, the 'monster' Glooskap is actually the centre of a morality tale, illustrating that while the gods might have the power to grant our desires, it is our responsibility not to present unworthy requests to them. For, as always, we must be careful what we wish for, especially in the presence of divine creatures.

Below: A tribesman performs a dance for his attentive family. Native American culture has very physical forms of expression, with each dance, song and artefact steeped in legend.

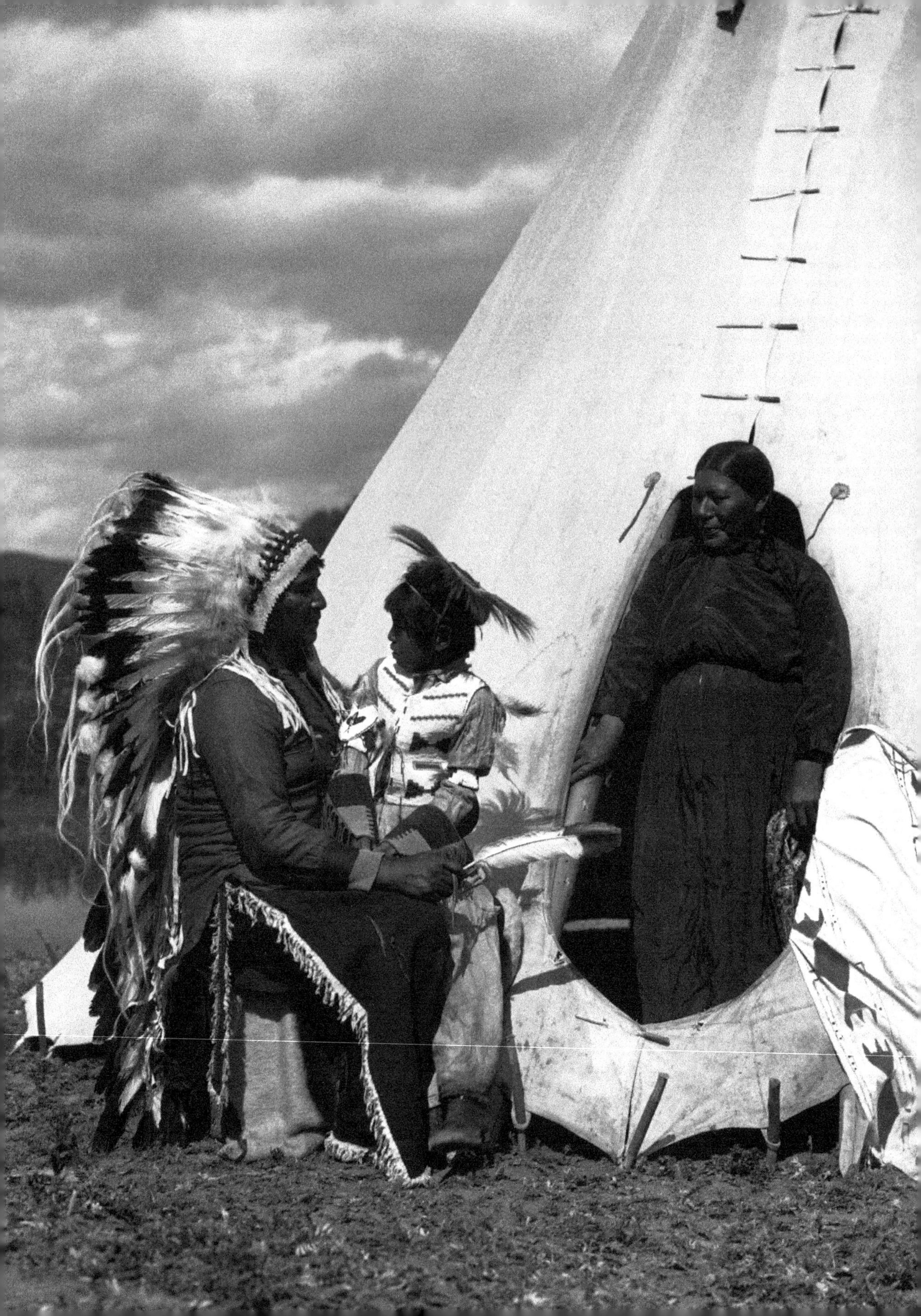

6

HUMANITY – LOVE, LIFE, MORALITY AND DEATH

It is always a point of interest that traditional Native American myths should be of continual curiosity to modern humans. The social life of modernity, particularly in urban environments, couldn't be further away from the belief systems, lifestyles and priorities of, say, a Plains Native American living under the wide-open skies of Dakota in the late 18th century.

IN MANY ways, however, it is the very difference between Native American mythologies, with their extremely strong sense of community, philosophical calmness and the central importance of nature, and the fractured and often angry ideas of modern urban society, that is part of their draw. When we read Native American myths and legends, there is something inherently calming and grounded about the worldviews that we encounter therein.

Left: A harmonious image of a Sioux family around their tipi. Tipis tended to be pitched in open land during the summer months, but among sheltered woodland in the winter months.

In many ways, this is not only due to the intrinsic humanity of the stories. As we have seen so far in this book, even narratives that deal with the greatest themes and figures – the creation of the world, or the whims and antics of the gods – always have a recognizably human element to them. They are, essentially, all tales about humanity, embracing the uncertainty, fickleness and heroism blended into the characters of people and society.

This chapter brings together a collection of stories that reflect the fundamental humanism of Native American myths and legends. Certain themes naturally predominate – kindness, difficult decisions, moral failings, the fear of death – but there is one theme above all that appears possibly more than all the others: the theme of love, and its close corollary, loss, which is where we begin.

THE BEREAVED MAN AND THE SPIRIT-WIFE (ZUNI)

This Zuni myth is one of beautiful profundity. It begins with a young man, stricken by grief following the death of his wife. He sat beside her grave, weeping night and day, inconsolable at the thought he would never see her again or hold her in his

Left: This grand photograph of a group of Sioux speaks of the loss of a great traditional culture in North America. In the second half of the 19th century, most Sioux were forced onto reservations.

Above: Set against a stunning backdrop of a Montana valley, a Sioux family offer up gifts to the dead in the tree grave above them. The bow and arrow indicate that the deceased was a hunter and warrior.

arms. Eventually the grief became too much, and he decided that he would go to the underworld itself – the Land of the Dead – to be with her.

So he made prayer sticks and uttered incantations over the grave, then waited until nightfall. In the dead of night, rising with a spectral light from the grave, the spirit of his wife appeared and sat down next to him. She looked at him with compassion, but also an aura of sadness. 'Do not be distressed', she said, 'for I have just crossed over from this world into the next.' The young man shook his head. 'I cannot live without you, and my love is consuming me, so much so that I need to go with you into the Land of the Dead.' Through her own love for her husband, the spirit-wife tried to change his mind, but it became clear that his desire was unmovable. Thus she said to him: 'If that is your wish then you can go with me, but a long journey is involved. Follow me, but know this – in the daylight hours I shall be invisible to you. For this reason, you will tie a red feather in my hair – it is this that you must follow in the daytime.'

So the man tied a red feather in his spirit-wife's hair and waited until the sun rose. As it did so, the form of his spirit-wife became fainter and fainter, until all that was left was the red feather hovering in the air. Then the feather appeared to rise and moved off through the landscape, heading towards the west. It moved quickly, so quickly that the man continually struggled to keep up as it crossed streams and rivers, went through woodland, floated up steep slopes and through villages. On occasions the man would call to his wife, telling her to slow down to allow him to catch up, which she did, although only for a moment before continuing onwards.

The journey continued over many days. For the man, it was a strange, harrowing time. On many occasions he lost sight of the feather, searching for it with rising panic. He would then catch a glimpse and set off again quickly, but with exhaustion drawing on his every step. Oftentimes he even wondered whether the feather was still connected to his spirit-wife, as it felt distant from him.

Then the feather eventually led him to a precipitous chasm. The man stopped on its edge, but the feather floated on gaily out across the void. He was at a loss in terms of what to do, but opted to climb down the side of the chasm. He eventually found himself on a narrow ledge, his feet struggling for purchase on the crumbling rock, and for a time it appeared that he would fall to his death. Yet he was saved in a curious manner. A squirrel raced up the rock towards him, and said, 'What are you doing? You do not have the powers to climb this cliff face. Let me help you.' And with that the squirrel took a seed from his cheek and planted it into a crevice in the rock. From the crevice magically sprouted a long, tough plant, which snaked its way across the chasm, forming a natural bridge that the man was able to use to cross over.

On the other side he spotted the feather, but now it was distant. Furthermore, it appeared to be heading towards an expansive lake. Nevertheless, the man's love compelled him to press on, but as he reached the edge of the lake he saw the feather disappear beneath the surface without so much as a ripple. He called his wife's name again and again, but it seemed and felt like she was gone forever.

Broken by distress, the man then heard the hoot of an old owl (traditionally

Below: This carved wooden spoon, from the Oneida Reservation in eastern Wisconsin, features a simple squirrel effigy on the handle.

> 'INSIDE IS A POWERFUL MEDICINE. IF YOU TAKE IT, YOU WILL FALL INTO THE DEEPEST SLEEP. WHEN YOU AWAKE, YOU WILL BE IN A DIFFERENT PLACE.'

associated with death and ghostly spirits). He looked up and saw the bird sat above him on a branch. The owl asked him why he was so sad, so the man explained everything. The wise owl spoke: 'Come with me, for I will show you how to be reunited with your wife once more.' The man followed the owl back to his home, where many other owls were. Only once inside, however, did the old owl reveal that beneath his appearance he actually had the form of a man.

Now the owl-man gave him the gift of a medicine bag, telling him: 'Inside is a powerful medicine. If you take it, you will fall into the deepest sleep. When you awake, you will be in a different place. Follow the sun until you reach a large anthill, and there your spirit-wife will be waiting for you. This time, as the sun comes up she will not disappear, but will instead become flesh once more, and you will be reunited. But note this. You will be eager to embrace her, but do not touch her until you have both returned to the village of your birth. If you attempt to hold her before that time, she will disappear forever.'

The man agreed and the owl-men performed the ritual. All unfolded as he had promised, and as the sun rose he found himself sat by the side of his beloved wife, who rose sleepily and somewhat confused. She smiled at her husband, saying, 'Your love for me is truly strong, as it has broken the bonds of death. We are meant to be together once more.'

So the couple now set off towards their village, the man keeping the appropriate distance away from her despite an overwhelming desire to enfold her in his arms. After four days of travel they came to Thunder Mountain, and it was there that the wife said she needed to stop and rest as she was exhausted from all the travelling, even though they were close to their pueblo.

Above: A carved figure of the owl-man. While in some legends the owl-man is benign, in others he is a predatory and evil character, given to carrying off humans for his food.

The man agreed, and they lay down next to one another, the man unable to take his eyes off the woman he loved.

It was while she slept that the man's longing overcame him. He just reached out with a single hand and touched his wife gently. At that moment she woke with a start and began to weep. 'What have you done?' she choked out. 'You couldn't resist, and now I will die again and you will lose me forever.' To the man's horror, his wife then dissolved until there was nothing but cold air in front of him. At that moment, an owl hooted from the tree, rhythmically repeating the words 'Shame! Shame! Shame!' The man continued his life, desolate forever.

Certainly, this myth is a reflection upon the consuming nature of love, which on occasions even strives to shatter death itself. But it is also a recognition that to defy death is an aberration, an unnatural attempt to reject the inevitable. Thus it is that the spirit-wife, as she floats across the landscape, almost seems careless of her husband's doting pursuit – with death, she has moved on.

Above: Photographic portraits of a Zuni man and woman. The latter wears heavy jewellery, made principally of sea shells and natural beads, indicative of her high status.

Above: In an Aleutian village, two men set out down the river in their *bidarka*, the shallow-draft vessels being perfect for negotiating rivers, lakes and coastal waters.

THE WIFE HUNT (ALEUT)

The pain and anguish of love resonates throughout many Native American myths, but so does the theme of the hunt for a suitable wife or husband. Oftentimes, an amorous young man would identify the woman of his dreams, but in his way stood obstacles and tests to prove that he was worthy of the woman's hand. A case in point comes from the Aleut, the people of the Aleutian Islands off the coast of Alaska, which explains why this myth has a particularly aquatic and coastal setting.

There once was a young man who desperately wanted to find a wife. During his childhood and adolescent years, he had been lonely and had spent most of his time developing his strength by lifting large stones, which became larger as he got older. So it was that by the time he set out in his hunt for a wife, he was confident that if he had to fight for her physically he could win.

The young man set out in a canoe across the seas, and eventually arrived at a village. He found somewhere to stay, where an attractive girl gave him food and a bed for the night. But the local men of the village felt threatened by the presence of the stranger, and thus they challenged the young man to a series of competitions with the strongest of their menfolk.

The first challenge was a hunt for beluga whale, the two men setting out to see who could bring back the biggest catch. After a day of furious hunting, the young suitor pulled in the biggest haul and was declared the winner of this particular competition. The following day the contest had an added seriousness. This time, the challenge was a boat race out on the water, with the young man pitted against a stocky villager. The race route took them around an island out in the bay; it would be a long test of endurance, and whoever got to the end first would be given a bow and arrow, which he would then fire at the loser as he approached the shore.

So that morning the two men set out, each of them paddling furiously with their oars, powering their *bidarkas* (canoes with a covering of animal skin) across the blue waters of the bay. After a time, however, the villager pulled ahead confidently, eventually getting so far in front of his opponent that they lost sight of each other. Indeed, the villager rowed at half pace, so confident was he that he would be the winner. Yet the newcomer had strange powers on his side. Using a magical incantation, he turned the canoe into a beluga whale, which took him down beneath the waves and swam underwater at such a rate that the man soon overtook his adversary, although the villager was not aware of the fact. As the young man neared the shoreline, he took the beluga back to the surface, where it turned once again into a boat, and he paddled ashore to victory.

The shock on the villager's face when he saw his opponent stood on the shore ahead of him was a sight to behold. Then within seconds an arrow struck his body, wounding him and standing as a very visible marker of his defeat. Furthermore, only the young man seemed to have the power to extract the arrow after being implored to do so by the village elders.

> USING A MAGICAL INCANTATION, HE TURNED THE CANOE INTO A BELUGA WHALE, WHICH TOOK HIM DOWN BENEATH THE WAVES.

Then came the third and final day of the competition. This time the young man faced a wrestling match with one of the most powerful men in the village. Combat would take place in a large ring, with the village crowded round to watch the men fight. In the centre of the ring, however, was a deep pit, full of rubbish and rotting meat. If either man could throw his opponent into this pit, then victory would be declared. The young man knew that if he could dominate his opponent, then the girl would be his.

It was a hard, brutal bout, each man trying to use a combination of strength and skill in an effort to overcome his opponent. Eventually, seizing a moment of opportunity, the young man bodily grabbed the villager and threw him into the pit and was proclaimed the winner.

Such was the status of the young man's victory that he was treated like a hero and given two wives and many items of wealth. And there the myth ends, rather strangely to our eyes, given that anything that has previously smacked of pride or vanity has tended to result in eventual punishment. Yet the young man is not arrogant, he is just victorious. The myth appears to celebrate the value of physical and moral strength, taking on all manner of obstacles to achieve the goals set in your imagination. After all, everyone loves a winner.

Above: An Aleut couple wearing their traditional costume, as seen in the 19th century. Being a people of the far northern coastal areas, their clothing needed to be warm and relatively waterproof.

OSSEO AND OWEENEE (ALGONQUIAN)

The Algonquian myth of Osseo and Oweenee works as a counterpoint to the previous legend. While the story of the young man competing for romantic victory celebrates physical valour, this myth is more about the rewards of moral virtue, from both those who possess it and for those who value it in others.

Oweenee was a young woman, one of 10 daughters of the tribal chief. She was the youngest and the most beautiful of all the daughters, but while her sisters spent much of their time reflecting and perfecting their physical beauty, Oweenee was generally distracted by other things. She loved to wander in the wilderness, and to seek out solitude and her own thoughts in the most inspiring of natural settings. Suitors came from far and wide to pursue the daughters' hands in marriage, and one by one the older girls were married off, encouraged by their parents. But Oweenee seemed largely uninterested in the men who paraded and postured in front of her, and thus she attracted the mockery and criticism of her family and the wider village. She didn't mind – she was an independent spirit to the core.

Also within the village lived Osseo. In contrast to Oweenee, Osseo was a worn-out and stumbling old man, his voice barely coherent and his shuffling stick-assisted gait mimicked cruelly by the young boys around him. Yet Osseo was a truly kind individual, wishing nothing but the best for all.

Left: The Algonquian village of Pomeiooc in North Carolina, illustrating how tribes with a more agricultural basis were free to build semi-permanent wooden structures.

One day, Osseo approached Oweenee and asked for her hand in marriage. Osseo saw through his age and failing health, perceiving the goodness that lay inside and she accepted the offer. Their marriage stunned the village, however. There was no other woman among them who had ever considered Osseo as marriageable material. Thus when they walked around the village, looking incongruous, others would make mocking comments. Oweenee didn't care – she had just committed herself to look after this old man until the day he died.

It was the time that the village celebrated the feast of the Evening Star (the planet Venus), and all the villagers gathered together and walked towards the site of the feast.

The walk was difficult for Osseo, not least because Oweenee's sisters kept muttering cruel comments, such as, 'Maybe he will fall over and break his neck, and spare my sister from being chained to him.' Yet on the way, Osseo kept pausing thoughtfully, looking up at the Evening Star and muttering prayers under his breath. One of the sisters overheard

OSSEO WAS THE SON OF THE KING OF THE EVENING STAR, ONCE A BEAUTIFUL MAN BUT WHO HAD BEEN CAST DOWN INTO DECREPITUDE BY AN EVIL SPELL.

Right: A depiction of Oweenee, the beautiful girl who gave her caring heart to an old man, Osseo, who was actually the youthful son of the King of the Evening Star.

his supplications; it was as if he was speaking to his father, which simply made them fear that he had lost his mind as well as his body.

Along the track, the group passed a large hollow log. All of a sudden, Osseo gave a loud cry to the heavens and dived into one end of it. All those around him wondered what was happening as he disappeared from view. Then, from the other end of the log emerged a young man, radiantly handsome, but still with the essential humanity of Osseo. For it was the case that in reality Osseo was the son of the King of the Evening Star, once a beautiful man but who had been cast down into decrepitude by an evil spell. Now the love of Oweenee had broken that spell – but at a terrible cost. For as Osseo leapt to his feet and ran back onto the track with a youthful stride, he watched as Oweenee herself shrivelled into old age, eventually supporting herself with the stick that just moments before had belonged to Osseo.

Now it was Osseo's turn to look after his wife, which he did with great tenderness and love. Eventually the pair made it to the feast, but it brought no joy for Osseo. Although he had

Above: Following Osseo's transformation back into a young, handsome man, Oweenee herself suffered from accelerated ageing, shuffling along using the stick that moments before had been Osseo's.

Above: An Algonquian ritual dance. Each dance would reflect the social structures of the tribe to varying degrees, dictating the nature of everyone's participation.

regained his youth, he was heartbroken to see what had become of his beloved Oweenee. Moreover, her transformation revealed the darkness that lay at the heart of others, particularly his bride's sisters. They became flirtatious with Osseo as they were captivated by his looks and physique, while they also secretly rejoiced that Oweenee had become physically ugly – now they would no longer be outshone by her beauty.

But then, cutting through the din of the feast, and eventually subduing that noise when all became aware of it, there came a strange song-like voice floating gently but clearly on the breeze. All at the feast were puzzled by the sound, but Osseo recognized it for what it was – the voice of his father. Eventually the words became clear: 'My son, you have suffered too much, and now is the time for the power of evil to be broken. You will leave this

Earth and come to live with me in heaven. All you have to do is eat the food that is in front of you, for it is blessed and will bring you all good things.'

So Osseo took up the food before him and ate, and in doing so the whole world around him was transformed. The tent in which they feasted began to lift from the ground, trembling as it did so, and ascended up towards the heavens. The common items on the table were transformed – wooden bowls and dishes became exquisite tableware made of silver and gold. The roof of the tent opened up to reveal a glittering starry sky. And what of the sisters and their husbands? They were turned into birds of various kinds, the men becoming vain robins, thrushes and woodpeckers, while the women became chattering magpies and blue jays. Oweenee and Osseo gathered all the birds and put them together in a silver cage.

For a moment the two lovers were scared, expecting that Oweenee herself would be reshaped into a bird. But instead, before his eyes, she once again took the form of her beautiful young self, wrapped in garments of supernatural colour and luminosity.

Slowly the tent and its occupants rose higher and higher until it reached the Kingdom of the Evening Star. There they were met by the King himself, overjoyed to have his son back, and now with a kind and worthy wife. But the King had a purpose for the couple and he summoned them before him, first telling them to hang the cage of birds over the entrance to his lodge. 'The evil that placed a curse upon you has been broken. Yet his evil dwells not far from here – he is the Small Star, also known as Wanebo, and he dwells in the lodge next to this one. His evil power is delivered through a beam of light that acts like a cruel bow and arrow, and you must

Below: Algonquian of North Carolina gather around a campfire. Such fires were often the first things built when a new camp was settled, providing cooking facilities but also a focal point for communal gatherings.

ANGER NOW STIRRED WITHIN THE BOY — TAKING HIS BOW, HE FIRED AN ARROW AT ONE OF THE BIRDS, CLIPPING IT SO THAT IT DROPPED TO THE GROUND BLEEDING.

be careful never to let that light fall upon you while you are here. Thankfully, the clouds have come to my aid and they shield my world partly from his wicked light.'

Oweenee and Osseo lived a blessed life in the Kingdom of the Evening Star, happy with each other and producing a handsome and inquisitive son. Although the boy wanted for nothing material as he grew up, he felt somewhat lonely, craving the stimulus of the people of Earth who his parents spoke about often. Once he was old enough, the boy's father gave him a small bow, with which he practised often and became a fine shot. Then one day the boy decided to open the silver cage, hoping that the birds would fly back to the Earth and take him with them. So he opened the cage door and out went the birds in a flurry. The boy called out to them, 'Take me with you!', but the birds seemed to fly on regardless. Anger now stirred within the boy – taking his bow, he fired an arrow at one of the birds, clipping it so that it dropped to the ground bleeding slightly. There, to his astonishment, the bird was transformed into a beautiful young woman.

But the boy had changed everything. By spilling blood in the heavens, he reversed the spell of ascent, and now he began to sink downwards as if pulled by gentle hands. Down and down he went, along with the lodge, until he and it came to rest on a large island upon the Earth. The birds came down with him, and as each landed back on the island they regained their human form. Yet the Evening Star, seeing what had happened, transformed them from mortal humans into a species of magical little people. The boy's parents, however, remained as they were, and they joined their son on the island to live for ever in each other's love.

To this day, fishermen who sailed around the island say they can still see the glittering lodge, shimmering in its heavenly glow, while they also witness the little people of the island dancing in celebration on the beach.

Below: An Algonquian couple of the 18th century. The heavy decoration on the paddle indicates that it is as much a ceremonial device as a practical tool.

Above: Cheyenne people gather for the sun dance. This major festival could take an entire year of planning and preparation, such was its sacred importance for the tribe.

THE MAN WHO MARRIED THE THUNDER'S SISTER (CHEROKEE)

The myth of Oweenee and Osseo is a haunting and somewhat ambiguous tale, split in its loyalties between Earth and heaven, as human beings often are spiritually. The one constant in the story is the love between Oweenee and Osseo, which transcends age and status and acts as a moral compass guiding the myth at all times.

Not all Native American myths of love and desire are so poetic and heart-warming, however. From the Cherokee, James Mooney collected the following myth, which begins with a classic tale of young love but then shifts into something rather sinister:

'In the old times the people used to dance often and all night. Once there was a dance at the old town of Sakwi'yi, on the head of Chattahoochee, and after it was well started two young women with beautiful long hair came in, but no one

THE POTLATCH FEAST

FEASTS AND CELEBRATIONS PUNCTUATED the Native American calendar regularly, these being held for various ritualistic, social and seasonal reasons. One of the most common types of feast among the tribes of the Northwest Pacific was the potlatch. In its most basic elements, the potlatch was a feast and gathering held to celebrate a special event, such as a birth, coming-of-age or wedding. But more than that, the potlatch was also a means by which the tribe established and reinforced its social hierarchy. The gift giving was, in a sense, competitive – all the guests swapped gifts among themselves, but the gifts had to be of equal or greater value than those that they received. Typical gifts were hunting weapons, oil, dried food, canoes and jewellery. By this form of exchange, the tribe established the status of the individual members; poor gift giving could signal a descent down the hierarchy, while ostentatious generosity ensured elevation.

This arrangement could be commercially problematic. Some families, sensing that

Above: A Tlingit woman, photographed in 1906, here wears the full ceremonial costume and face paint of the potlatch festival.

their status was rocky, might borrow possessions as a loan, using these to demonstrate a wealth that they actually did not possess, further pushing them into poverty. This factor, along with other cultural reasons, led to the 19th century white governments condemning the practice. Indeed, in 1884 an amendment of the Indian Act of 1876 stated that: 'Every Indian or other person who engages in or assists in celebrating the Indian festival known as the "Potlatch" or the Indian dance known as the "Tamanawas" is guilty of a misdemeanor, and shall be liable to imprisonment for a term not more than six nor less than two months in any gaol or other place of confinement; and any Indian or other person who encourages, either directly or indirectly, an Indian or Indians to get up such a festival or dance, or to celebrate the same, or who shall assist in the celebration of same is guilty of a like offence, and shall be liable to the same punishment.' The Draconian ban was never effective, however, and the law was finally rescinded in 1951.

Below: Alaskan peoples gather for the potlatch. Each participant had to have sufficient wealth to bring tradeable goods.

knew who they were, or whence they had come. They danced with one partner and another, and in the morning slipped away before anyone knew that they were gone; but a young warrior had fallen in love with one of the sisters on account of her beautiful hair, and after the manner of the Cherokee had already asked her through an old man if she would marry him and let him live with her. To this the young woman had replied that her brother at home must first be consulted, and they promised to return for the next dance seven days later with an answer; but in the meantime if the young man really loved her, he must prove his constancy by a rigid fast until then. The eager lover readily agreed and impatiently counted the days.

'In seven nights there was another dance. The young warrior was on hand early, and later in the evening the two sisters appeared as suddenly as before. They told him their

Below: On a Cherokee reservation in North Carolina in 1888, a dance is held before a ball game. The Cherokee had a variety of ball games, some of which were quite violent, incurring injuries among the participants.

brother was willing, and after the dance they would conduct the young man to their home, but warned him that if he told anyone where he went or what he saw he would surely die.

'He danced with them again and about daylight the three came away just before the dance closed, so as to avoid being followed, and started off together. The women led the way along a trail through the woods, which the young man had never noticed before, until they came to a small creek, where, without hesitating, they stepped into the water. The young man paused in surprise on the bank and thought to himself, "They are walking in the water; I don't want to do that." The women knew his thoughts just as though he had spoken and turned and said to him, "This is not water; this is the road to our

T̲HEY DANCED WITH ONE PARTNER AND ANOTHER, AND IN THE MORNING SLIPPED AWAY BEFORE ANYONE KNEW THAT THEY WERE GONE...

house." He still hesitated, but they urged him on until he stepped into the water and found it was only soft grass that made a fine level trail.

'They went on until the trail came to a large stream, which he knew for Tallulah river. The women plunged boldly in, but again the warrior hesitated on the bank, thinking to himself, "That water is very deep and will drown me; I can't go on." They knew his thoughts and turned and said, "This is no water, but the main trail that goes past our house, which is now close by." He stepped in, and instead of water there was tall waving grass that closed above his head as he followed them.

'They went only a short distance and came to a rock cave close under Ugun'yi (Tallulah Falls). The women entered, while the warrior stopped at the mouth; but they said: "This is our house; come in and our brother will soon be home; he is coming now." They heard low thunder in the distance. He went inside and stood up close to the entrance. Then the women took off their long hair and hung it up on a rock, and both their heads were as smooth as a pumpkin. The man thought, "It is not hair at all," and he was more frightened than ever.

'The younger woman, the one he was about to marry, then sat down and told him to take a seat beside her. He looked, and it was a large turtle, which raised itself up and stretched out its claws as if angry at being disturbed. The young man said it was a turtle, and refused to sit down, but the woman insisted that it was a seat. Then there was a louder roll of thunder and the woman said, "Now our brother is nearly home." While they urged and he still refused to come nearer or sit down, suddenly there was a great thunder clap just behind him, and turning quickly he saw a man standing in the doorway of the cave.

'"This is my brother," said the woman, and he came in and sat down upon the turtle, which again rose up and stretched out its claws. The young warrior still refused to come in. The

> THE HUNTER WAS TERRIBLY FRIGHTENED, AND SAID: 'THAT IS A SNAKE; I CAN'T RIDE THAT.'

brother then said that he was just about to start to a council, and invited the young man to go with him. The hunter said he was willing to go if only he had a horse; so the young woman was told to bring one. She went out and soon came back leading a great *uktena* snake that curled and twisted along the whole length of the cave. Some people say this was a white *uktena* and that the brother himself rode a red one. The hunter was terribly frightened, and said: "That is a snake; I can't ride that." The others insisted that it was no snake, but their riding horse. The brother grew impatient and said to the woman: "He may like it better if you bring him a saddle, and some bracelets for his wrists and arms." So they went out again and brought in a saddle and some arm bands, and the saddle was another turtle, which they fastened on the *uktena*'s back, and the bracelets were living slimy snakes, which they got ready to twist around the hunter's wrists.

Below: A wedding party of the Kwakwaka'-wakw (an indigenous people of the Pacific Northwest), with the bride sat in the centre, accompanied by musicians.

'He was almost dead with fear, and said, "What kind of horrible place is this? I can never stay here to live with snakes and creeping things." The brother got very angry and called him a coward, and then it was as if lightning flashed from his eyes and struck the young man, and a terrible crash of thunder stretched him senseless.

'When at last he came to himself again he was standing with his feet in the water and both hands grasping a laurel bush that grew out from the bank, and there was no trace of the cave or the Thunder People, but he was alone in the forest. He made his way out and finally reached his own settlement, but found then that he had been gone so very long that all the people had thought him dead, although to him it seemed only the day after the dance. His friends questioned him closely, and, forgetting the warning, he told the story; but in seven days he died, for no one can come back from the underworld and tell it and live.'

Above: Photographed on his wedding day in 1906, an Ute groom wears his finest ceremonial clothing. By this point in history, the Ute were living on three large reservations.

This myth turns from a potentially humorous tale of romantic attraction into a grim drama of ghastly creatures and eventual death. If there is a warning here, it is about pursuing love blindly wherever it might lead.

THE BEAR FOSTER-SON (INUIT)

As the final myth of this chapter, we turn away from tales of underworld horror to a legend that is far more humane, albeit with a poignancy and a deep sense of mortality beneath. This is the myth of the Bear Foster-Son, as told by the Inuit people living in the icy landscape north of the Arctic Circle.

A long time ago, there lived an old woman whose home was by the edge of the freezing sea. She was especially well known by the local hunters, who moved along the shoreline before going out fishing or while pursuing their prey, and they often stopped on the way back from their expeditions to give the old woman gifts of meat and blubber.

One day, the hunters stopped by and told her of an orphan bear cub on the shoreline, wondering if she wanted to take it in. Moved by the animal's plight, she went out and gathered up the poor creature, which was terribly cold and filthy. Once the animal was inside, the woman cleaned it up, warmed it in front of the fire and fed it with hearty food. Little did she know then, but she had gained a friend for life.

So it was that the bear grew up alongside humans, learning their ways and thinking as they did. The one problem, however, was that the growing bear had a physical strength far beyond that of the humans he associated with. So it was that the old woman cautioned the bear when he was young, telling him to sheathe his claws when playing with the children around him.

So he played with the children for many years, but eventually his strength reached levels that always resulted in the children crying from the rough-and-tumble. Now he was approaching adulthood, however, the hunters of the village recognized that having a bear accompany them on a hunt could be to their

Left: A relatively modern photograph of an Inuit family. They still wear the traditional *Annuraaq* clothing, made from skin and fur and being both warm and waterproof.

advantage – the bear's physical senses of hearing and smell were far greater than anything possessed by a human, and his strength and speed were awesome to behold. He was also an expert at catching seals, clawing them out through holes in the pack ice. The bear therefore became one of the hunters, a valued member of his human pack. But venturing out far and wide brought its problems. On one occasion when the men were close to another tribe's land, the bear was nearly killed by rival hunters who mistook him for prey. Thus when the men got back to the village, they asked the old woman to make the bear some sort of distinguishing headgear that would tell hunters far and wide that this bear was special and should be left alone. So the old woman made the bear a broad collar of plaited sinews, which he wore around his neck.

Yet despite this precaution, the hunters of the other tribes began to take an interest in the bear, with some warriors boasting that if they saw it they would kill it, although others cautioned against such actions, knowing the bear's close connection with the old woman. Nevertheless, the old woman was painfully aware that the bear must not do anything to bring it into conflict with humans. She told the bear: 'Whenever you meet humans, wherever they are from, welcome them and do not threaten them. Only if they attack you must you attack them back'.

One time, during a black and stormy night, the bear came back from a hunt later than usual. He ambled into the house and sniffed the old woman, as if urging her to rise. She went outside the house and there found the body of a dead man, a warrior from another tribe. She quickly summoned the menfolk of the village into conference. By the appearance of the body, the man had been killed when fleeing the bear, peeling off his clothes as he ran in terror. It became apparent that he had attacked the bear, wanting this legendary animal as a trophy, but instead he had roused the bear's defensive instincts and was killed. Nevertheless, now that the bear had slain a human, his own life would forever be in danger if he stayed in the village.

The old woman, foster-mother to the bear for so many years, spoke gently to him: 'Though it breaks my heart to say this,

Above: An Inuit dancing bear carved in soapstone.

you must leave. If you stay here with me, I fear that you will be killed, and I could not stand that. You should go out and rejoin the world of bears.' The bear understood what was being said and knew that it was true. But for a long time the bear and the old woman stayed with their heads pressed against one another, tears silently tumbling down their faces.

The next morning was bright and sunny, and the bear and the old woman said their final tender goodbyes before the bear turned and prepared to step out into the future. Before he did so, the woman surreptitiously dipped her hands in oil and wiped a black mark along the bear's flank to mark him out from the other creatures and to protect him from hunters by making his coat less desirable to them. And so the black-marked bear loped off across the ice, never forgetting the woman who raised him.

The story of the bear's foster-mother is emotionally powerful. It illustrates how from the hearts of humans, even in those of hunters, mercy and kindness can flow to the most vulnerable of creatures. But life being what it is, emotions must always be balanced with pragmatism, as cruel as that might seem.

Below: The old woman reluctantly says goodbye to her bear foster-son.

BLACKFOOT MARRIAGE CUSTOMS

THE 19TH CENTURY ANTHROPOLOGIST George Bird Grinnell made some of the most detailed studies of Blackfoot society and culture. Here he describes some of the social rules surrounding marriages:

'As a rule, before a young man could marry, he was required to have made some successful expeditions to war against the enemy, thereby proving himself a brave man, and at the same time acquiring a number of horses and other property, which would enable him to buy the woman of his choice, and afterwards to support her.

'Marriages usually took place at the instance of the parents, though often those of the young man were prompted by him. Sometimes the father of the girl, if he desired to have a particular man for a son-in-law, would propose to the father of the latter for the young man as a husband for his daughter.

'Sometimes, if two young people are

fond of each other, and there is no prospect of their being married, they may take riding horses and a pack horse, and elope at night, going to some other camp for a while. This makes the girl's father angry, for he feels that he has been defrauded of his payments. The young man knows that his father-in-law bears him a grudge, and if he afterwards goes to war and is successful, returning with six or seven horses, he will send them all to the camp where his father-in-law lives to be tied in front of his lodge. This at once heals the breach, and the couple may return. Even if he has not been successful in war and brought horses, which of course he does not always accomplish, he from time to time sends the old man a present, the best he can.

'Notwithstanding these efforts at conciliation, the parents feel very bitterly against him. The girl has been stolen. The union is no marriage at all. The old people are ashamed and disgraced for

Far left: A Native American couple. In Blackfoot marriage traditions, the pressure was on the courting male to prove he was worthy of the woman.

Above: The fertility god Kokopelli, generally depicted playing a flute, was a lively and mischievous figure, who could bring life to plants and animals as much as childless couples.

their daughter. Until the father has been pacified by satisfactory payments, there is no marriage. Moreover, unless the young man had made a payment, or at least had endeavored to do so, he would be little thought of among his fellows, and looked down on as a poor creature without any sense of honor.'

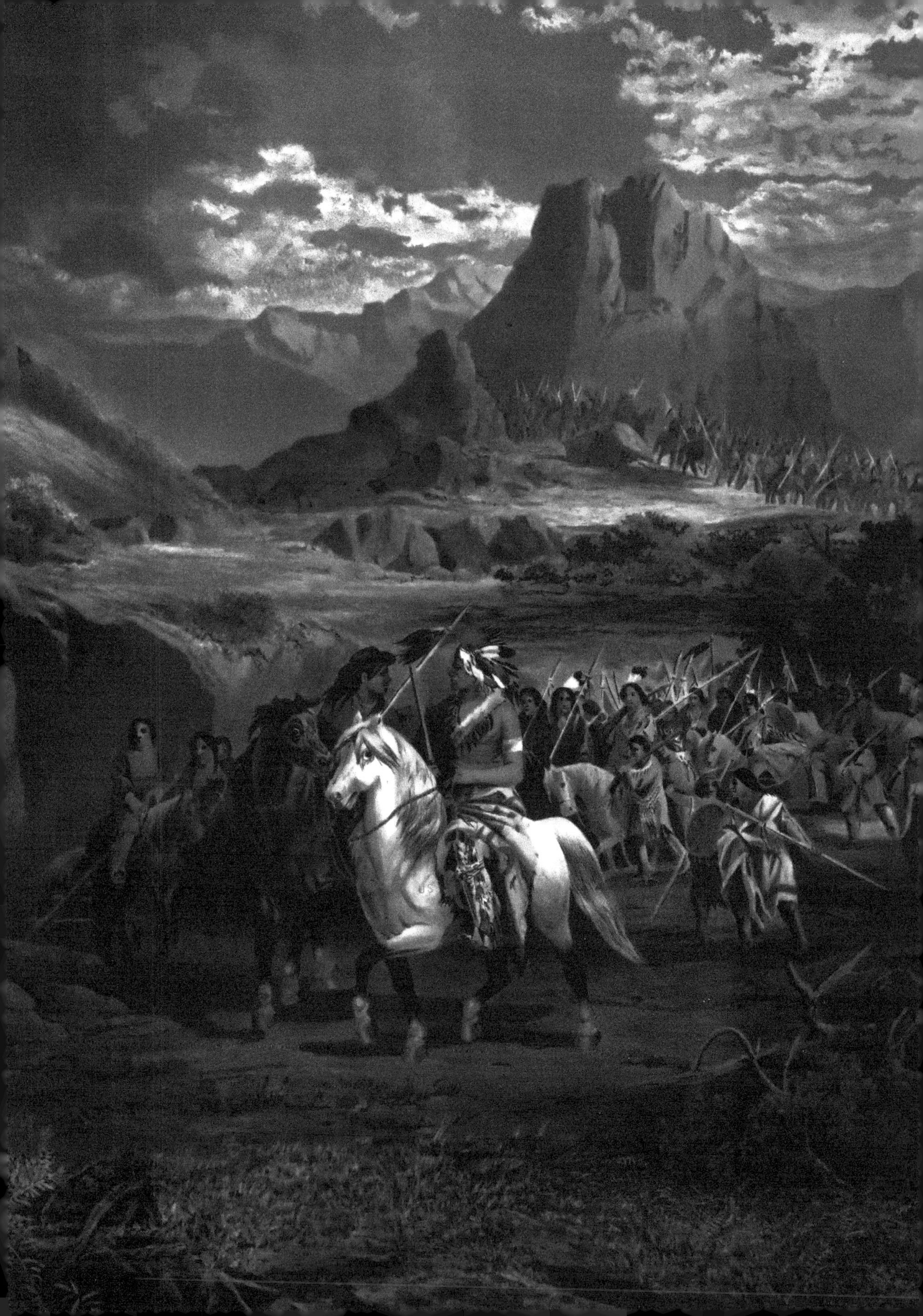

7
WARRIOR RACE

The Native Americans were a warlike people. When honour was slighted, territory or food supplies threatened or if revenge was to be had, many tribes would fight with a ferocity that was terrifying to behold. Almost every male in a village would be raised learning how to use a spear and a bow (and later a rifle) for hunting purposes, acquiring skills that would be transferrable to the battlefield.

FURTHERMORE, WHEN ROUSED in anger the tribal warriors could be merciless in their violence, applying various forms of slaughter to vanquished enemies. Looking past the brutality, we should not misrepresent the warrior ethos of the Native Americans, not least because that ethos could vary from tribe to tribe or even from village to village. Generally, the Native American 'way of war' was not a matter of attempting to wipe your enemies from the face of the Earth with 'total war' – that was more the martial philosophy of modern powers – but to inflict a severe enough localized defeat to establish supremacy and to satisfy pride. Being hunter-gatherer or subsistence agriculture people, with a finely balanced

Left: A sizeable Indian war party moves forward into action. Note how a large number of the warriors are on foot; horses were rarely available for every single member of a war party.

Below: A Lenni Lenape warrior. Note his recurved bow, the shape of which added extra power while keeping the length of the bow manageable.

relationship to survival, it was not in the Native American interest to wage a long war of attrition with anyone. Rather, their warrior practices were based more on raiding, ambushes and symbolic victories, although on occasions certain tribes fielded armies of several thousand men.

In this chapter, we will see a range of myths surrounding the practice, culture and the tragedy of war. These myths show a people capable of martial aggression when required and with an appreciation of the warrior spirit, but they do not celebrate mindless belligerence and murder, for such was an affront to nature.

THE GRASSHOPPER WAR (LENNI LENAPE)

The Lenni Lenape people were indigenous to the northeastern woodland areas of the United States and Canada, roughly running from present-day New Jersey up into the Lower Hudson Valley. Their story of the 'Grasshopper War' is short, simple and salutary, and illustrates how humanity's tendency towards making war is in many ways inherent in nature itself. Note that the teller of the tale, an Indian elder, did not regard it as myth, but as an event that actually occurred back in local history.

A long time ago, there were two villages separated by a large lake. Although the lake stood as a physical barrier between the two communities, there was no social barrier. The peoples of the villages regularly crossed the water in their canoes to meet or to go on shared hunting trips. Wives met with wives and children with children, and all was harmonious.

One particular day, children from both villages were playing together on one side of the lake. A boy who came from the other side of the water looked down on the grass and spotted a grasshopper sat there in the sun. But this was no ordinary grasshopper, for it was unusually large and robust – a super-grasshopper. The boy immediately scooped it up and made it into his own personal pet. All the other children gathered around him, impressed by this fine specimen.

Then the problems began. One boy from the village grew jealous of the creature. He thought to himself: 'Why should this boy get to keep the grasshopper? After all, it was found on our territory. I therefore have a right to claim it.' So the boy swiftly grabbed the grasshopper, an action that immediately set off a furious argument between the children of the two villages. The argument spiralled out into a physical fight, with punches and kicks being exchanged. The noise of the fight brought out the women of both villages from their lodges – the menfolk were out hunting – and on finding their children cut, bruised and distressed, they also started to row among themselves, and this altercation also blew up into physical violence.

Eventually the men of the two villages returned from their hunt to find their wives and children in a distraught state. Each side told its own version of the story, and the true cause of the incident was entirely lost. But now the warriors of the two villages felt aggrieved and swore vengeance on each other. The two communities separated back across the lake. Now the only people who crossed the water were war parties raiding the other tribe, fighting and killing.

It went on in this way for many seasons. Eventually, the reason for the rift emerged in all its triviality, but by then it was too late – the tribes of the lake would never again be friends.

THE FALSE WARRIORS OF CHILHOWEE (CHEROKEE)

The legend of the "Grasshopper War" speaks eloquently about how the burning flames of conflict can be fanned from the smallest of sparks. On other occasions, however, war came as a genuine response to acts of tribal aggression. Another story from the Cherokee oral histories collected by James Mooney illustrates

Above: An Indian youth practises the skills of archery. A well-trained bowman was perfectly capable of hitting small, even moving, targets at more than 100m (330ft).

Above: A portrait of Ca-Ta-He-Cas-Sa-Black Hoof, a principal chief of the Shawnees, the portrait painted in 1837. The chief of any tribe had to exhibit a warrior nature, inspiring all those under him to acts of bravery.

such an occurrence, and does so in a narrative that dramatically cranks up the rising tension between two tribes:

'Some warriors of Chilhowee town, on Little Tennessee, organized a war party, as they said, to go against the Shawano. They started off north along the great war trail, but when they came to Pigeon river they changed their course, and instead of going on toward the Shawano country they went up the river and came in at the back of Cowee, one of the Middle settlements of their own tribe. Here they concealed themselves near the path until a party of three or four unsuspecting townspeople came by, when they rushed out and killed them, took their scalps and a gun belonging to a man named Gunskali'ski, and then hurriedly made their way home by the same roundabout route to Chilhowee, where they showed the fresh scalps and the gun, and told how they had met the Shawano in the north and defeated them without losing a man.

'According to custom, preparations were made at once for a great scalp dance to celebrate the victory over the Shawano. The dance was held in the townhouse and all the people of the settlement were there and looked on, while the women danced with the scalps and the gun and the returned warriors boasted of their deeds. As it happened, among those looking on was a visitor from Cowee, a gunstocker, who took particular notice of the gun and knew it at once as one he had repaired at home for Gunskali'ski. He said nothing, but wondered much how it had come into possession of the Shawano.

'The scalp dance ended, and according to custom a second dance was appointed to be held seven days later to give the other warriors also a chance to boast of their own war deeds. The gunstocker, whose name was Gulsadihi', returned home to Cowee, and there heard for the first time how a Shawano war party had surprised some of the town people, killed several and taken their scalps and a gun. He understood it all then, and told the chief that the mischief had been done, not by a hostile tribe, but by the false men of Chilhowee. It seemed too much to believe, and the chief said it could not be possible, until the gunstocker declared that he had recognized the gun as one he had himself repaired for the man who had been killed. At last they were convinced that his story was true, and all Cowee was eager for revenge.

'It was decided to send ten of their bravest warriors, under the leadership of the gunstocker, to the next dance at Chilhowee, there to take their own method of reprisal. Volunteers offered at once for the service. They set out at the proper time and arrived at Chilhowee on the night the dance was to begin. As they crossed the stream below the town they met a woman coming for water and took their first revenge by killing her. Men, women and children were gathered in the townhouse, but the Cowee men concealed themselves outside and waited.

'In this dance it was customary for each warrior in turn to tell the story of some deed against the enemy, putting his words into a song which he first whispered to the drummer, who then sang with him, drumming all the while. Usually it is serious business, but occasionally, for a joke, a man will act the clown or sing of some extravagant performance that is so clearly impossible that all the people laugh. One man after another stepped into the ring and sang of what he had done against the enemies of his tribe. At last one of the late war party rose from his seat, and after a whisper to the drummer began to sing of how they had gone to Cowee and taken scalps and the gun, which he carried as he danced. The chief and the people,

Below: An Indian drummer. Drums were beaten for a variety of ceremonial purposes, including war preparations, and were often regarded as containing the spirit of the animal used to make the drum skin.

Right: Drums could be regarded as near-sacred objects in many tribes. A drum keeper, often the eldest son of a high-status family, might be appointed to watch over a particularly important instrument.

'WE THOUGHT OUR ENEMIES WERE FROM THE NORTH, BUT WE HAVE FOLLOWED THEM AND THEY ARE HERE!'

who knew nothing of the treacherous a[ ] laughed heartily at what they thought was a great joke.

'But now the gunstocker, who had been waiting outside with the Cowee men, stripped off his breechcloth and rushed naked into the townhouse. Bending down to the drummer – who was one of the traitors, but failed to recognize Gulsadihi' – he gave him the words, and then straightening up he began to sing, "*Hi!* Ask who has done this!" while he danced around the circle, making insulting gestures toward every one there. The song was quick and the drummer beat very fast.

'He made one round and bent down again to the drummer, then straightened up and sang, "*Yu!* I have killed a pregnant woman at the ford and thrown her body into the river!" Several men started with surprise, but the chief said, "He is only joking; go on with the dance," and the drummer beat rapidly.

'Another round and he bent down again to the drummer and then began to sing, "We thought our enemies were from the north, but we have followed them and they are here!" Now the drummer knew at last what it all meant and he drummed very slowly, and the people grew uneasy. Then, without waiting on the drummer, Gulsadihi' sang, "Cowee will have a ball play with you!" – and everyone knew this was a challenge to battle – and then fiercely: "But if you want to fight now my men are ready to die here!"

'With that he waved his hand and left the townhouse. The dancers looked at each other uneasily and some of them rose to go. The chief, who could not understand it, urged them to go on with the dance, but it was of no avail. They left the townhouse, and as they went out they met the Cowee men standing with their guns ready and their hatchets in their belts. Neither party said anything, because they were still on friendly ground, but everyone knew that trouble was ahead.

'The Cowee men returned home and organized a strong party of warriors from their own and all the neighbouring Middle settlements to go and take vengeance on Chilhowee and on Kuwa'hi, just below, which had also been concerned in the raid. They went down the Tennessee and crossed over the mountains, but when they came on the other side they found that their enemies had abandoned their homes and fled for refuge to the remoter settlements or to the hostile Shawano in the north.'

Much is revealing about this legend, not least for providing an insight into some of the ritual, feasts and etiquette surrounding

Below: A photograph of a lake in Chilhowee, Tennessee, taken in the early 20th century. Chilhowee is the Cherokees' traditional homeland.

Below: The figure of Periska-ruhpa, of the Gros Ventre tribe. The Gros Ventre name is a French label, but the tribe was also known as the A'ani, A'aninin, Haaninin and Atsina.

Native American warrior culture. The most brutal part is undoubtedly that of the killing of the innocent pregnant woman, an act that alienates most modern readers from the story. Yet putting such responses aside for a moment, there is something horribly logical and formulaic about this killing, the Cowee seeing it as just deserts for the betrayal by the Chilhowee. And while the Cowee gather their men ready for violence, the real battle is enacted by intimidation and threat, not by actual blows, resulting in a near-bloodless victory for the Chilhowee. As we noted at the beginning of this chapter, a major conflict of the 'total war' variety was rarely a part of the warrior psyche – widespread destruction was, after all, rarely to anyone's benefit.

THE CROW NECKLACE (GROS VENTRE)

Another collection of myths speak of the conflicted loyalties produced by the Native American practice of taking prisoners during raids and wars, the prisoners either becoming slaves or, on occasions, integrating into the lives of their captors. The myth of the Crow Necklace is a prime example of this type of legend. It comes from the Gros Ventre, an Algonquian-speaking Native American tribe located in north-central Montana. The story revolves around one particular boy. Born of the Assiniboine, this boy was captured as an infant by the Gros Ventre and taken into their tribe as a slave. As he grew up, he demonstrated a warrior's spirit, body and acumen, and his status changed from slave to that of valued hunter and fighter. Time also shifted his loyalties and he participated in several battles against the Assiniboine, including one in which he shot and wounded two men with arrows – these

Left: An Assiniboine camp painted around 1850. Note how the woman attaches a travois to a dog; canines were commonly used to pull small loads, before horses became more accessible.

men were his brothers. It seemed clear that in all ways he now identified with the Gros Ventre, who called him Crow Necklace.

One day, Crow Necklace and a group of others were ambushed by an Assiniboine war party while they were down at an old camp by the river. It was a short, brutal battle and the Gros Ventre party was outnumbered. Some of them managed to escape, including Crow Necklace, but when he had put distance between him and his opponents he discovered that his sister was missing, likely taken by the Assiniboine. The sister was not a blood relative – she was part of the Gros Ventre family to which the young man now belonged – but he knew that he could not abandon her.

> ONE DAY, CROW NECKLACE AND A GROUP WERE AMBUSHED BY AN ASSINIBOINE WAR PARTY WHILE THEY WERE DOWN AT AN OLD CAMP BY THE RIVER.

So Crow Necklace turned around, and drawing upon all the stealth he had learned as a hunter he circled back and crept up on the Assiniboine village, moving silently among the tipis in the dead of night. Eventually he came upon one tipi from which men's voices were heard. Peeping through a gap in the fabric, he saw none other than his birth father and his two brothers, the ones he wounded in battle. Steeling his

Above: A Gros Ventre camp, featuring spectacular family-sized tipis, but with the flag of the United States leaving no doubt as to who is in charge of the land.

courage, he wrapped himself in a large cloak to disguise his features, then entered the tipi, where his father – unaware of the identity of the stranger now in their midst – invited him to sit down and share a pipe. This the young man did, but after a while he finally revealed his identity to those present, slipping off the cloak and saying, 'Father, it is I.'

Thus began a family reunion of mixed and strong emotions. He even confessed to his brothers that it had been him who had shot them in battle, an occurrence that they found to some degree amusing and understandable. He also asked about the whereabouts of his sister. His father therefore called together a celebratory feast known as the scalp dance, which all the slaves of the village attended. He could not spot his sister among them, however, although he recognized many others from the Gros Ventre.

Because of the arrival of Crow Necklace and his hunt for his sister, his father had declared that the tribe would not move on to another ground for four whole days. Yet now, Crow Necklace's actual loyalties began to reveal themselves. Knowing that the Assiniboine would eventually move on, taking the Gros Ventre slaves further away from their tribal homes, he secretly advised them to escape, telling them to store meat for the journey and to make moccasins from pieces of their tipis. On the last night of the four days they made their escape at night, Crow Necklace going with them. Following Crow Necklace's advice, they fled in a direction the Assiniboine would not expect, eventually hiding in the reeds by the side of a frozen lake.

At daybreak, the Assiniboine discovered the flight of the slaves and sent out search parties to find them, but they found no one, even when they surveyed the lake around which the slaves were expertly hiding. Crow Necklace sought to help the fugitives in any way he could, even killing a lone Assiniboine warrior who looked as if he might happen upon the hidden people.

For four days the Gros Ventre slaves moved on with Crow Necklace at their head, who guided their movements during the dark and helped them hide in the daylight hours. On the way, he received guidance from a family of owls about the direction to take and his eventual destination. The owls also used their magic to help the fugitives find copious amounts of food, the spirits themselves setting traps for the prey animals. Such was the volume of the catch that they had a surfeit of food, which they eventually took back to the Gros Ventre village. The celebrations

CROW NECKLACE SOUGHT TO HELP THE FUGITIVES, EVEN KILLING A LONE ASSINIBOINE WARRIOR WHO LOOKED AS IF HE MIGHT HAPPEN UPON THE HIDDEN PEOPLE.

Below: Assiniboine warriors attack another Indian camp. Camp raiding was one of the most common forms of inter-tribal violence, producing short, brutal actions with limited casualties.

when they returned were euphoric, and Crow Necklace was fêted by the whole tribe. He married one of the chief's daughters and became a master in the art of medicine, using it to summon the spirits that brought them food on the journey. He also ultimately knew that his physical and spiritual home would forever more be with the Gros Ventre.

The Crow Necklace myth is a story of homecoming. It is psychologically involving on many levels, not least because of its intersection with the classic nature vs. nurture debate, in which it eventually seems to come down cleanly on the side of the latter, at least in terms of tribal and familial loyalties. But it does present a certain masculine bond between warriors of both tribes, the two brothers accepting that the other brother shot them not out of malice, but through performing his duty as a warrior.

THE SIOUX MAIDEN WARRIOR (WHITE RIVER SIOUX)

Most of the Native American myths about conflict tend to focus on men, the gender traditionally associated with hunting and war. On occasions, however, the narrative folds outwards to embrace warrior women, who step into the shoes of men quite naturally and with an equal skill and spirit.

A case in point comes from a legend told by one Jenny Leading Cloud, a member of the White River Sioux living in the Rosebud Indian Reservation, South Dakota, in the 1960s. She

Left: Sioux warriors gather on horseback ready to ride out to fight. The long lances were as much hunting weapons as fighting tools, being ideal for killing buffalo at the gallop.

gave the account to Richard Erdoes, a compiler and reteller of Native American myths and legends (see Richard Erdoes and Alfonso Ortiz, *American Indian Myths and Legends*: Pantheon Books, 1984), and it is striking how it captures the essence of Native American warrior culture.

There was once a Sioux chief called Tawa Makoce ('His Country'), who exhibited all the traits one would want from a chief – fearless in battle, wise in giving advice, generous with his time and spirit. Tawa Makoce had four children – three sons and a daughter – and while Tawa Makoce himself was a superb warrior, his sons had less fortune on the battlefield. They were strong, brave and sought to impress their father, but too often they made fatal tactical mistakes and one by one they were killed in the Sioux battles against the Crow Indians. The chief grieved their loss and consoled himself in the love of his daughter.

> EVENTUALLY THE SIOUX WAR PARTY FOUND WHAT THEY WERE LOOKING FOR – A HUGE CROW CAMP CONTAINING HUNDREDS OF WARRIORS...

Now that daughter was called Winyan Ohitka, meaning 'Brave Woman'. She had a strong spirit and was physically beautiful. Many men approached her with marriage propositions, but she rejected them all. Instead of following the path of marriage and domestic peace, she instead wanted to 'count coup' (demonstrate her bravery in battle) on the Crow enemy as revenge for the death of her three brothers.

The opportunity came all too soon when the Sioux were compelled to ride out to face a large Crow war party. Winyan Ohitka went to her father and told him that she would also ride into action with the men, a declaration that made his heart swell with pride although he was stricken with fear that his last remaining child would die in battle. He gave her a charmed war bonnet to wear, a fine horse to ride and all her brothers' weapons, then told her to go.

And so Winyan Ohitka went to war with the menfolk, her heart flushed with excitement mixed with fear. Alongside her were two men in particular, Red Horn and Little Eagle. They couldn't have been more different characters. Red Horn was

Above: A Salish woman on horseback. Accounts from 18th- and 19th-century observers describe the Native Americans as natural riders, with exceptional command over the animals.

confident and charismatic, the son of a chief and had made marriage proposals to Winyan Ohitka on numerous occasions, riding out each rejection. By contrast, Little Eagle was – when it came to matters of the heart – a shy young man. He was also deeply in love with Winyan Ohitka, but he kept his desires to himself and never declared them to her.

Eventually the Sioux war party found what they were looking for – a huge Crow camp containing hundreds of warriors, far more than they had in their own party. But now was not the time for faint hearts, and Winyan Ohitka stirred the Sioux to attack without fear. To Red Horn she gave her eldest brother's lance, and to Little Eagle she gave her second brother's bow and arrow, imploring both of them to use the weapons to count coup upon the enemy. As she went into battle, the only thing she carried was her father's coup stick (a decorative staff that is used to touch the enemy chief to demonstrate the owner's bravery).

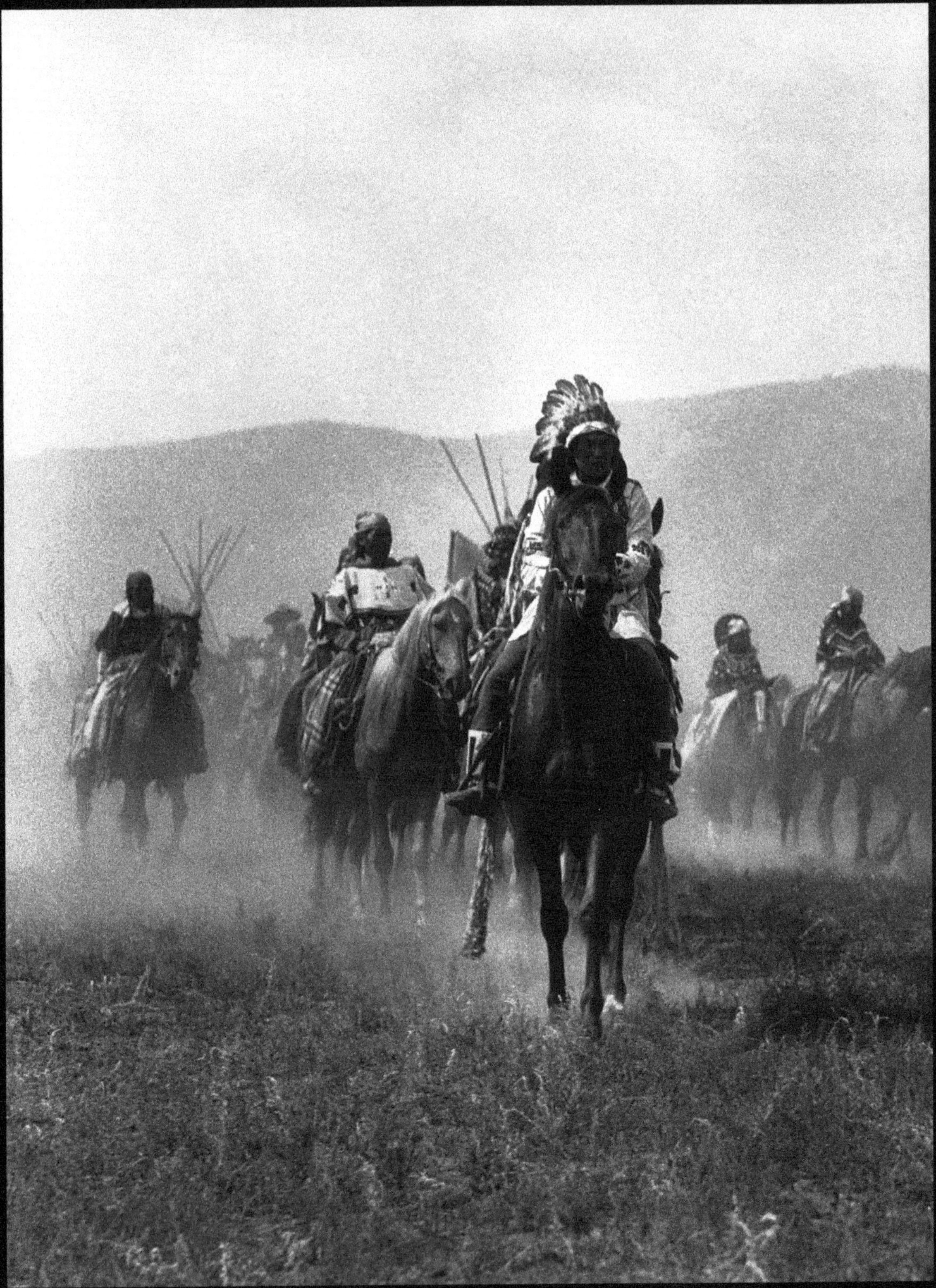

Winyan Ohitka thundered into the heart of the melee, counting coup on all sides. The menfolk, seeing one of their women ride in a blaze of bravery, pushed themselves to achieve ever-greater victories over their enemies. Yet the odds were still stacked against them in terms of numbers. Then, the air whistling with arrows, spears and bullets, Winyan Ohitka's horse fell, throwing her to the ground. Red Horn, seeing her plight, nevertheless rode past her, pretending that he had not witnessed what happened. Little Eagle, by contrast, rode through the smoke and dust to her side, dismounted, and gave her his own horse. The horse had been wounded, and was not strong enough to carry two people, hence Little Eagle was almost certainly sacrificing himself for his love. Winyan Ohitka protested – 'I can't leave you here to die!' – but Little Eagle smacked the horse's rear with his bow and off it galloped, leaving Little Eagle to fight on foot.

The conflict eventually drew to its dire end, the field littered with the bodies of the fallen. Yet it had been a Sioux victory, one that freed them from the fear of the Crow for generations and which secured their tribal lands. Red Horn survived, but with shame – his bow was broken and he was sent home. And what of Little Eagle? He died in battle, fighting with astonishing and selfless bravery. Winyan Ohitka and her father recognized that this man had likely saved her life. Little Eagle's horse was sacrificed to serve him in the afterlife, and his body was laid high up on a scaffold in a place of great honour. Winyan Ohitka, her eyes open to the type of man Little Eagle was in reality, grieved for him for the rest of her life and never married.

In the background of this myth, we get a sense of the sheer brutality and energy carried within a Native American tribal battle. Those who survive are scarred by the experience, marked by loss, but there is the undoubted sense in which Winyan Ohitka helped inspire the male warriors to even greater heights of bravery, whatever the final cost to themselves.

> THE CONFLICT EVENTUALLY DREW TO ITS DIRE END, THE FIELD LITTERED WITH THE BODIES OF THE FALLEN.

Far left: A tribe of Kootenai, from the state of Idaho, on the move. Note how these riders have stirrups; such riding tack, plus saddles and bits, was adopted from the Europeans.

COUNTING COUP

COUNTING COUP IS A military practice distinctive to Native American warfare, with little in the way of equivalents among other global systems of warfare. Counting coup was most associated with the people of the Great Plains and Great Basin/Plateau regions, although it was found to varying degrees across North America. In essence, counting coup involved touching an enemy with the hand or a specially designed coup stick, and then escaping unharmed. Note that the enemy is not actually wounded or killed in this action; the coup-counting warrior is simply demonstrating his bravado, bravery and skill, and therefore accruing prestige. A warrior who regularly counted coup had a high status among his peers. Further acts of counting coup included stealing the enemy's horses or weapons from beneath his nose.

Coup sticks are particularly fascinating and revered objects of Native American history. These were long wooden sticks but heavily decorated with feathers, fur, scalps, bones and other items. Thus transformed, the coup stick had a magical status with powers akin to that of a wand.

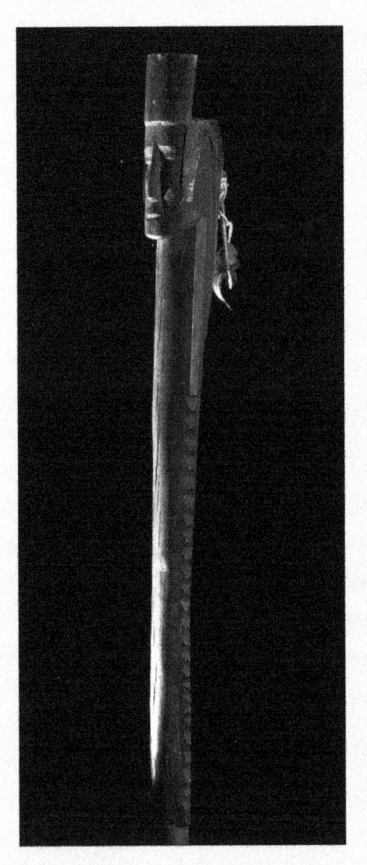

Above left: A coup stick carved with a human face. This stick is relatively plain, the decoration mainly coming through carving rather than adornment.

Above right: A more highly decorated coup stick. Notches were carved into the wooden parts of the handle whenever coup was counted.

HEAD CHIEF AND YOUNG MULE (CHEYENNE)

The myth of the Sioux Maiden Warrior introduces us to the practice of counting coup, an ingredient of Native American warfare that is unusual to modern eyes (see feature box). To reiterate the significance of counting coup in the warrior's psyche, we turn to the northern Cheyenne legend of Head Chief and Young Mule. What is particularly poignant about this legend is that it is embedded in truth, events that actually happened in the late 19th century as the Native American way of life was virtually destroyed by the encroachment of the white colonizers and settlers.

The legend is set in September 1890, by which time the Cheyenne found themselves in depressing reservations, squeezed out of their traditional spaces by the white men. Within the reservations life was very hard. There was little to do, and there was also little to eat; the land was not rich in food, and such had been the slaughter of the buffalo by the white settlers that this traditional source of food and hide was almost entirely absent. (In the 1600s there were likely some 30 million buffalo roaming the American plains, but by the end of the 19th century there were only a few hundred left alive. Some US policymakers actually saw the destruction of the buffalo as a means to drive the Native Americans to the point of extinction.)

On the reservation was Head Chief and his loyal follower Young Mule. One day, Head Chief decided enough was enough. Accompanied by Young Mule, he ventured beyond the boundaries of the reservation to hunt for his people. Although this was illegal in the eyes of

Below: Officials of the US government meet with Sioux and Cheyenne peoples on a reservation in the 1890s. The reservations often had little of the rich hunting lands previously enjoyed by the tribes.

the white men, for Head Chief the wider ancestral lands still belonged to his tribe, the Cheyenne, so he was perfectly within his rights to hunt there.

During the hunt, they found no buffalo, but they did find a cow in a field. Head Chief shot the cow with his rifle and butchered it on the spot. On the way back to the reservation, their horses heavily laden with meat, they unexpectedly met the young nephew of the man who owned the cow. This man, spotting the beef, immediately understood what had happened. Head Chief, sensing the trouble that lay ahead for his people, shot the young man and killed him, burying his body on the land. He and Young Mule then took the meat back to the reservation.

Some weeks passed as the law enforcement investigated the disappearance of the man. Eventually they found the body and tracked the trail back to Head Chief, who was accused and convicted of murder, then sentenced to death.

Now the law enforcement officers had a problem. Head Chief was a senior figure among the Cheyenne, and there was

Below: An Indian warrior with his fighting lance. Such lances typically measured about 1.5m (5ft) in length, and were used mainly as thrusting weapons, although they could also be thrown.

the possibility that his execution could lead to a local uprising. Despite this, justice had to be done. It was Head Chief himself who came up with the solution. Above all, he wanted to die like a warrior and not as a criminal, so he chose his own method of execution. He instructed all the police officers, armed with their guns, to form a line on an open patch of ground. There, Head Chief would run at them, counting coup with his coup stick while they attempted to shoot him. His death would be inevitable, but at least he would die on his feet and with honour. Furthermore, the rest of the tribe would watch the event, seeing the tragedy unfold but restrained by watching a tribal custom being played out.

> HEAD CHIEF, SENSING THE TROUBLE THAT LAY AHEAD FOR HIS PEOPLE, SHOT THE YOUNG MAN AND KILLED HIM, BURYING HIS BODY ON THE LAND.

The local police chief recognized that it made more sense to follow Head Chief's request than to risk a revolt, so he did as the old Indian said and lined his men up with their weapons. Then Head Chief starting to run, counting coup among the policemen as they took shots, trying not to hit each other or the bystanders. But then Young Mule also joined in, himself preferring a noble death to life imprisoned on the reservation. So both men counted coup until, inevitably, they were brought down by the police bullets and lay dead in the dust. In memory of the two men, local people tied the feathers from Head Chief's magnificent headdress to a rock, where they remained for many years.

THE ATTACK ON THE GIANT ELK (JICARILLA APACHE)

There is another thread of Native American martial myths, ones that delve back into days seemingly beyond time, populated by warring creatures and contending elements as much as by human players. These tales are far more fantastical in their nature, but their reflections upon violence and the 'way of the warrior' are just as incisive. We see this in the Attack on the Giant Elk, as told by the Jicarilla Apache of New Mexico.

The myth is set in the time of monsters, when humans existed but lived fraught lives, preyed on by species of giant animals, particularly the Giant Elk and the Great Eagle. The humans implored the gods to send them help in their battle against these creatures and they received Jonayaiyin, a young man with divine ancestry. Jonayaiyin was a warrior through and through, whose crusade it was to fight battles on behalf of humankind. He decided that his first mission was to track down and kill Giant Elk, his main weapons being powerful arrows given to him by his mother.

Jonayaiyin's mother had told him that Giant Elk was to be found in an expanse of desert lying to the south. Jonayaiyin made the arduous journey there, and from a vantage point on top of a large hill he eventually spotted Giant Elk stood alone in the middle of a plain. The warrior realized that this would not be an easy kill. There was no cover on the plain that Jonayaiyin could use to approach to within shooting distance – no trees, no bushes, no rocks. At that moment a lizard appeared before him, enquiring about what he was doing. Jonayaiyin explained all and the lizard offered to help. The creature suggested that Jonayaiyin don the discarded skin of the lizard and use that natural camouflage to get close to the Elk. Thus Jonayaiyin struggled into the lizard skin. Next a gopher joined the discussion and also offered his assistance. The gopher, using his powerful limbs, dug underground, creating a long tunnel until he popped up beneath the Elk itself. Then he proceeded to nibble away at the Elk's fur beneath his chest, cutting away a bald patch directly over the massive thumping heart. The Elk looked down at the gopher and said, 'What are you doing?' The gopher replied: 'I am cutting a few hairs for my little ones; they are now lying on the bare ground.' Giant Elk bought the answer, and when the gopher was finished he crawled back through the tunnel to Jonayaiyin: 'I have cut away a circle of fur over Giant Elk's heart. You must shoot there to kill the creature. You can also use the tunnel that I have dug to advance without being seen.'

Above: The Jicarilla Apache Vash Gon, one of the many individuals photographed by Edward S. Curtis. His hair is braided and wound with strips of deer skin.

Above: Elk petroglyphs dating back hundreds of years speak of the importance of this animal for Native American tribes. An Elk carcass would provide food, clothing and bone tools.

So Jonayaiyin set off down the tunnel in a state of fear and excitement, and eventually he emerged beneath Giant Elk as planned. He saw the circle of bare skin with the heart beating behind it, and into that spot Jonayaiyin fired four arrows, penetrating Giant Elk's heart. But the great beast was not killed so easily. He rose in anger, and as Jonayaiyin now fled back down the tunnel, Giant Elk tore through the earth with his magnificent antlers, attempting to catch the fleeing assassin. Such was the volume of soil he threw up that entire mountain ranges were formed in the process. Magical spiders of various colours and from each point of the compass came to Jonayaiyin's assistance, throwing up ultra-strong webs across the hole and slowing Giant Elk's progress. Eventually he succumbed to his wounds and to exhaustion, and eventually he collapsed and died.

It was a great victory for Jonayaiyin. He skinned the body of Giant Elk and made himself a fine coat from the hide. As rewards to lizard and gopher, he gave them the front quarters and the hindquarters respectively; the antlers – those that had destroyed the ground – he took back to his village as a trophy of his adventure, and as weapons to use in the future. For there remained a further challenge ahead – Great Eagle, also known as I-tsa. Jonayaiyin's mother, using her powers of vision, told him where to find this creature, and Jonayaiyin reached there in four giant bounds across the land.

> AS JONAYAIYIN FLED BACK DOWN THE TUNNEL, GIANT ELK TORE THROUGH THE EARTH WITH HIS MAGNIFICENT ANTLERS, ATTEMPTING TO CATCH THE FLEEING ASSASSIN.

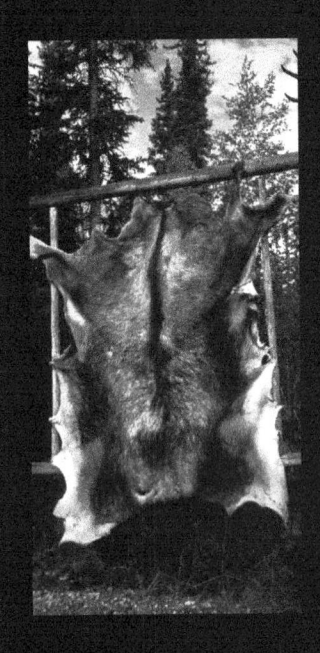

Above: An elk hide is stretched across a drying rack. The hide would be made into jackets, trousers and footwear, and also sacks for holding goods. Sinew was used for rope and for bow strings.

Far right: A Native American eagle catcher. The eagle catcher would collect eagle feathers, regarded as sacred objects, without harming the revered bird itself.

I-tsa's home was atop a giant rock, and in the nest she had two eaglets always hungry for food. The rock nest was beyond the powers of human access, so instead Jonayaiyin stood out in the open, presenting himself to be picked up by Great Eagle and carried to the eyrie. So I-tsa spotted Jonayaiyin and rushed down four times to attempt to grab him. For the first three times, Great Eagle failed to grab Jonayaiyin – the tough coat of Giant Elk's hide prevented the eagle's talons from penetrating Jonayaiyin's body. On the fourth attempt, however, the claw caught up in the coat's laces and Jonayaiyin was carried aloft and dropped into the nest.

The eaglets gathered around him to feast, then one of them shouted: 'He is still alive!' 'Nonsense,' said the mother bird, 'that is just the air escaping from where my talons have pierced him.' And with that she flew off without stopping to check whether Jonayaiyin was truly dead or alive. Once I-tsa had left, Jonayaiyin threw some of Giant Elk's blood on the floor of the nest for the eaglets to feast on, thus distracting them. He then asked when their mother would return. 'In the afternoon when it rains,' they answered. So Jonayaiyin readied himself. He carried with him one of Giant Elk's antlers, a weapon of great power. When Giant Eagle returned at the stated time, Jonayaiyin rose up and rammed the tip of the antler into her back, piercing the armour of feathers and killing the huge bird instantly. Then Jonayaiyin asked the eaglets as to what time their father would return. 'Our father comes home when the wind blows and brings rain just before sunset,' they said. Again Jonayaiyin prepared himself, gripping the antler with violent intent. The giant father-bird appeared as predicted, but carrying a distraught woman with an infant on her back. As the eagle approached the nest, he dropped his human load, who were dashed to death on the rocks below. Furious with the desire for revenge, Jonayaiyin again struck with the antler, killing the predatory bird with a single blow. Then Jonayaiyin killed both of the eaglets so that they would not grow up full of a desire for revenge. At this moment, the power of the eagles over humans was broken, although as a parting curse they bestowed rheumatism upon the human race.

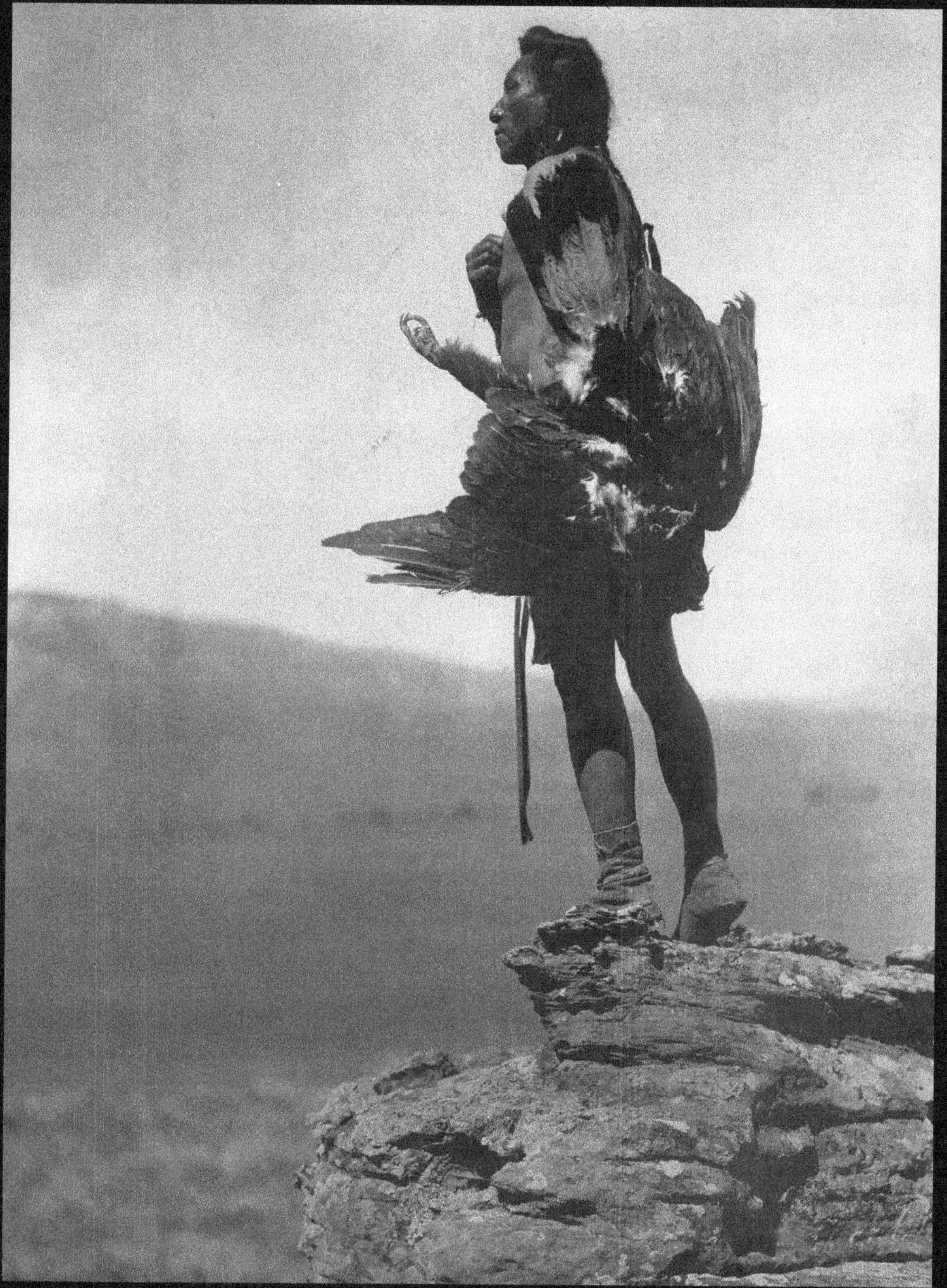

Jonayaiyin's victory over the giant animals is a myth of human ascent in the order of things, but also a reflection on the Native American way of war. Note how in both the actions, cunning, camouflage, observation and deceit play their part, all key ingredients in effective warfare. Nature is also used to gain an advantage. What matters in Jonayaiyin's world is the end result, not the way of getting there.

CHIEF HOOK NOSE (WHITE RIVER SIOUX)

The historical narrative of the Native Americans during the 19th century is an especially sad one, as they were robbed progressively of their lands, often at the end of a gun barrel. We have already seen an instance – Head Chief and Young Mule – of a warrior myth that speaks of the clash between the indigenous people and the colonizers. We end this chapter on a similar note, the White River Sioux myth of Chief Hook Nose, which also speaks eloquently and sadly of this time. What is especially moving about this short story is the way that Hook Nose eventually realizes that he cannot fight for victory, but he can fight for nobility.

The myth speaks about a chief of the Cheyenne – allies of the Sioux – called Hook Nose on account of his distinguished facial feature. Hook Nose was a warrior of legendary feats and indefatigable bravery, fearless in action and feared by his enemies. Hook Nose also used great medicine, a sacred stone and magical war paint – applied to both himself and to his horse – that made him immune to bullets fired from the guns of his enemies. It was critical, however, that before a battle Hook Nose avoided touching any metalware when eating, otherwise the medicine would be fatally weakened.

One day, Hook Nose responded to news that a group of Cheyenne were locked in battle with a force of white solders. He stirred his warriors to action, and together they ate a hasty meal before riding out to battle. In the rush, Hook Nose touched metal implements. He recognized the fact, but this was no time

Above: An Alaskan tribal eagle head. Eagles held a prestigious place in the Native American cultures, representing values such as courage and leadership, but also acting as messengers between heaven and earth.

> HE STIRRED HIS WARRIORS TO ACTION, AND TOGETHER THEY ATE A HASTY MEAL BEFORE RIDING OUT TO BATTLE.

for timidity – having eaten, he leapt onto his horse and led his warriors forward into battle.

The fight was a terrible one. The white soldiers were using the latest rifles, which were quick-firing and highly accurate, so casualties among the Cheyenne were heavy. The terrain was also difficult for the tribal warriors, as the white soldiers were firing from a sandspit island in the middle of a deep river. When the Indians waded into the river on their horses to confront them, they were slowed by the water and thus became perfect targets for the enemy riflemen. Nevertheless, Hook Nose prepared to ride fearlessly against the enemy. An old warrior next to him cautioned: 'Hook Nose, today you have touched metal things, thus your medicine will not protect you against the enemy's bullets. You should purify yourself for four days and then fight'. But Hook Nose was undeterred. 'No, the fight is now, not in four days. If I die, at least I will die a warrior. Only the rocks and mountains live forever.' And with that he galloped down to the enemy defences, where he was hit by a bullet in the chest and died.

The body of Hook Nose was taken up by his fellow warriors and carried from the battlefield, the Cheyenne even breaking off the fighting to honour their great leader. The village went into mourning, but all understood that Hook Nose had stayed faithful to his ideal of the warrior spirit, preferring death on the battlefield to safety at home.

Above: The death of Hook Nose in battle. He died fearless in war, an act that would ensure he also became part of the tribe's ancestral mythology, and a legend for future warriors.

SELECT BIBLIOGRAPHY

Arcturus Publishing. *Native American Myths & Legends*. London: Arcturus Publishing, 2017.

Erdoes, Richard and Alfonso Ortiz (eds). *American Indian Myths and Legends*. New York: Pantheon Books, 1984.

Ferguson, Diana. *Native American Myths and Legends*. London: Collins & Brown, 2001.

Jackson, Jake. *Native American Myths*. London: Flame Tree, 2014.

Lewis, Jon E. (ed.). *A Brief Guide to Native American Myths and Legends*. London: Constable & Robinson, 2012.

Linderman, Frank Bird, Marie L. McLaughlin and Katharine Berry Judson. *Native American Myths and Legends: Collections of Traditional Stories from the Sioux, Blackfeet, Chippewa, Hopi, Navajo, Zuni and Others*. St Petersburg, FL: Red and Black Publishers, 2013.

McNab, Chris. *The Native American Warrior 1500–1890*. New York: Thomas Dunne, 2010.

INDEX

Page numbers in *italics* indicate illustrations.

Abenaki tribe 146, 159–63
afterlife myths
  Blue Jay and Ioi 112–16
  the Double-Faced Ghost 119–20
  the Elk-Charmer 120–6
  Mondawmin 102–8
  the *Nunne'hi* 108–11
  the Skeleton House 126–31
  Yunwi Tsunsdi (Little People) 132–3
Aleut tribe 172
  clothing 174
  the Wife Hunt 172–4
Algonquian tribe 48–9, *180*
  campfires 179
  Osseo and Oweenee 174–80
  ritual dances 178
  settlement 175
  Wendigo 148–50, 151
Anishinaabe group 48–9, 144–6
Arapaho tribe 72
  buffalo hunts 77
  Chief Goes-In-Lodge 74
  the Splinter-Foot Girl 72–8
Arikara tribe 66
Arrow Boy 58–64
Assiniboine tribe 202–6, *203*, *205*
Attack on the Giant Elk, the 215–20

Bear Family, the 66–9
Bear Foster-Son, the 188–91
bears 15, 66–9, 188–91
Bella Coola tribe 41
Bereaved Man and the Spirit Wife, the 167–71
Blackfoot tribe
  Blackfoot Genesis and the Origins of Marriage 47–54
  hunting 51
  marriage customs 192–3
  medicine man 53

Blue Jay and Ioi 112–16
Bridge of the Gods, the 96–9, *98*
Brule Sioux tribe 85
buffalo hunting *see* hunting
burial rituals 123, *133*

Ca-Ta-He-Cas-Sa-Black Hoof, Chief *198*
Chenoo 146–8
Cherokee tribe *201*
  ball games 184
  Chief Sequoyah 79
  the Crane and the Hummingbird 79–81
  dances 184
  David Vann 108
  dress 80
  the False Warriors of Chilhowee 197–202
  the Man Who Married the Thunder's Sister 181–8
  the *Nunne'hi* 108–11
  Nun'yun'wi, the Stone Man 150–6
  the origins of natural medicine 64–6
  the Owl Gets Married 86–7
  Stand Waite 111
  Yunwi Tsunsdi (Little People) 132–3
Cheyenne tribe 213
  Arrow Boy 58–64
  Chief Hook Nose 220–1
  the Double-Faced Ghost 119–20
  dress 119
  Head Chief and Young Mule 211–15
  medicine man 59
  rituals 59, 62, 181
Chief Hook Nose 220–1
Chinook tribe 112–16, *114*
Chippewa tribe 48, 88, *103*
  Chief May-Maush-Kow-Aush *105*
  Chief Pee-Che-Kir 89
  Mondawmin 102–8
  Opechee the Robin 88–93
  Seven Fires Prophesy 48–9
  the Water Panther 144–6

  wedding ceremony 92
clothing 37, 51, 57, 58, 80, 96, 102, 119, 126, 174, 189
Coast Salish people 96
compass points, importance of 30
corn festivals 131
counting coup 212, 213–15
Coyote and Cougar 32–5
Coyote and Fox in Disguise 81–6
coyotes 10–12, 21, 32, 32–5, 81–6
Crane and the Hummingbird, the 79–81
creation myths
  Coyote and Cougar 32–5
  The Four Mounds 13–17
  Ladder Through the Four Worlds 18–22
  the Lakota creation story 28–31
  The Master of Life 9–12
  the Raven and the Light of the World 31–2
  Sky-Mother and Sky-Father 36–41
  the Turtle and the Twins 23–8
Crow Necklace, the 202–6

Dakota Sioux tribe 87
dances 178, 184
  ghost dances 87, 101, 102, 113, 119
  sun dance 181
directionality, importance of 30
Double-Faced Ghost, the 119–20
dress 37, 51, 57, 58, 80, 96, 102, 119, 126, 174
drums 199, 200
dwellings
  lodges 10, 34
  tipis 17, 47, 55, 57, 204
  wickiups 17
  wigwams 107

eagles 41, 84, *84*, 217–18, *218*, 220
Earth-Mother 36–41, *39*
Elk-Charmer, the 120–6
elks 120–6, 215–20, *217*, *218*

INDEX

False Warriors of Chilhowee, the 197–202
family, myths concerning *see* culture myths
Four Mounds, The 13–17
funeral scaffolds 123

ghost dances *87, 101, 102, 113, 119*
Glooskap 159–63
gods and monsters, myths concerning
   Chenoo 146–8
   Glooskap 159–63
   Nun'yun'wi, the Stone Man 150–6
   Pamola 156–9
   the Sky Spirit 136–40
   the Thunderbird 140–4
   the Water Panther 144–6
   Wendigo 148–50, *151*
Goes-In-Lodge, Chief *74*
Grasshopper War, the 196–7
Great Spirit, the *28*, 28–31, *47*
Great Vulture *21*
Grinnell, George Bird *50, 50*, 192
Gros Ventre tribe
   the Crow Necklace 202–6
   Periska-ruhpa *202*
   tipis *204*

Haida tribe *31*, 31–2
Hastobiga *61*
Head Chief and Young Mule 211–15
Hewitt, I.W.B. 23
Hopi tribe
   directionality 30
   dress *126*
   hunting *44*
   kachina dolls *83*
   Ladder Through the Four Worlds 18–22
   rituals *18, 19, 19, 131, 132*
   rock paintings *129*
   shaman *20*
   the Skeleton House 126–31
   snake priests *131*
humanity, myths concerning
   the Bear Foster-Son 188–91
   the Bereaved Man and the Spirit Wife 167–71
   the Man Who Married the Thunder's Sister 181–8
   marriage customs 192–3
   Osseo and Oweenee 174–80
   the Wife Hunt 172–4
hunting *44*, 51, 51–3, *52*, 54, 65–6, *72*, 72–8, 77, 78, 157

Indian Removal Bill (1838) 109
Inuits 188–91, *189*
Iroquois tribe 9, 84–5

Jemez Pueblo tribe *154*
Jicarilla Apache tribe 13–17, *14*, 215–20
   tipis *17*

Vash Gon *216*
wickiups *17*

kachinas (benign spirits) 20, *21*, 83
Kangi (the crow) 29
kivas 19, *19*
Kokopelli *193*
Kootenai tribe *211*
Kwakwaka'wakw tribe *187*

Ladder Through the Four Worlds 18–22
Lakota tribe *28*, 28–31
Lenni Lenape tribe *196*, 196–7
lodges *10, 34*
Loowitlatkla (Lady of Fire) 96–9

Man Who Married the Thunder's Sister, the 181–8
Mandan tribe *13, 34*
marriage 54–8, 86–7, 192–3
   wedding ceremonies *143, 187, 188*
masks *21, 41, 93, 139, 151, 152*
Master of Life, the 9–12
May-Maush-Kow-Aush, Chief *105*
medicine bundles 62, *63, 64,* 66
medicine men *43*, 53, 59, 59–64, *61, 105*
medicine, natural 64–6, *65, 66,* 69
Mississaugas tribe 48–9
Mondawmin 102–8
Mooney, James 79, *79*, 86, 108, 109, 111, 132, 152, 181, 197
musical instruments *125, 199, 200*

Nakoaktok tribe *152*
natural world, myths concerning the
   the Bridge of the Gods 96–9
   Coyote and Fox in Disguise 81–6
   the Crane and the Hummingbird 79–81
   the 'Everything-Maker' 84–5
   Opechee the Robin 88–93
   the Origin of the Mosquito 93–5
   the Owl gets married 86–7
   the Splinter-Foot Girl 72–8
Navajo tribe *61*
   artwork *30, 39, 136*
   directionality 30
   shaman *69*
Nez Perce tribe 81–6
Nunne'hi, the 108–11
Nun'yun'wi, the Stone Man 150–6

Odawa tribe 48–9
Ojibwa tribe *103*
   Mondawmin 102–8
   the Water Panther 144–6
   wigwams *107*
Ojibwe tribe 48–9, 144–6
Oji-Cree tribe 48–9
Old Man, the 47–58
Oneida tribe *169*

Opechee the Robin 88–93
Origin of the Mosquito, the 93–5
Osseo and Oweenee 174–80
Owl Gets Married, the 86–7
owls 15, *40*, 84–7, *86, 87, 120*, 169–70

Pamola 156–9
Pawnee tribe *102, 141*
Pee-Che-Kir, Chief *89*
Penobscot tribe *68*
   the Bear Family 66–9
   Glooskap 159–63
   hunting *157*
   Pamola 156–9
people *see* culture myths; humanity, myths concerning
Periska-ruhpa *202*
petroglyphs *see* rock carvings
Piegan Blackfeet tribe
   the Old Man and marriage 54–8
   tipis *55, 57*
   trade blankets *58*
Pima tribe
   earth lodges *10*
   the Master of Life 9–12
   rock carvings *11*
Pomo tribe *32*, 32–5
Potawatomi tribe 48–9
potlatch feast *152, 182*, 182–3, *183*
Pueblo tribe
   artwork *20*
   directionality 30
   and eagles *84*
   rituals *21*
Puyallup tribe 96–9

Rabbit Boy 44–7
rabbits *44*, 44–7, *45*, 85
Raven and the Light of the World, the 31–2
ravens *31*, 31–2, 85, *85*
Red Jacket *27*
robins 88–93
rock paintings *11, 24, 32, 38, 44, 72, 112, 129, 145, 158, 217*

Salish tribe *209*
sand paintings *39, 136*
Sat Sa *37*
Seneca tribe 23–8, *27*
Sequoyah, Chief *79*
Seven Fires Prophesy, the 48–9
shaman 20, *69*
Shawnee tribe *198*
Sioux Maiden Warrior, the 207–11
Sioux tribe *87, 137, 167, 207, 213*
   Chief Hook Nose 220–1
   the Elk-Charmer 120–6
   ghost dance *101*
   offerings *168*
   Rabbit Boy 44–7

the Sioux Maiden Warrior 207–11
the Thunderbird 140–4
tipis *47, 165*
Skeleton House, the 126–31
Sky Spirit, the 136–40
Sky-Mother and Sky-Father 36–41
snake priests *131*
soapstone carvings *190*
Spider-Grandmother 20, 22
spirit realm *see* afterlife myths
Splinter-Foot Girl 72–8
stone carvings *23*
sweat lodges 88–93, *91*

Thunderbird, the 140–4
tipis *17, 47, 55, 57, 165, 204*
Tlingit tribe
 actor's mask *93*
 the Origin of the Mosquito 93–5
 potlatch feast *182*
 shaman's rattle *144*
 warriors *95*
'Trail of Tears' *110*
tree carvings *76*
Tsimshian tribe *141*

Turtle and the Twins, the 23–8
turtles 28–31, *29*

underworld myths 12–21
Ute tribe *188*

Vann, David *108*
Vash Gon *216*

Wabanaki Confederacy 146–8, 159–63
Waite, Stand *111*
war, myths concerning
 the Attack on the Giant Elk 215–20
 Chief Hook Nose 220–1
 the Crow Necklace 202–6
 the False Warriors of Chilhowee 197–202
 the Grasshopper War 196–7
 Head Chief and Young Mule 211–15
 the Sioux Maiden Warrior 207–11
Water Panther, the 144–6
wedding ceremonies *143, 187, 188*
Wendigo 148–50, *151*
White River Sioux tribe *207*
 Chief Hook Nose 220–1

Rabbit Boy 44–7
the Sioux Maiden Warrior 207–11
tipis *47*
wickiups *17*
Wife Hunt, the 172–4
wigwams *107*
wolves 81–6, *83*
wooden carvings *23, 31, 83, 120, 141, 169, 170, 212, 220*

Yunwi Tsunsdi (Little People) 132–3

Zuni tribe
 the Bereaved Man and the Spirit Wife 167–71
 dress *171*
 natural medicine *65*
 owl effigy *86*
 rock carvings *38*
 Sat Sa *37*
 Sky-Mother and Sky-Father 36–41
 stone carvings *23*
 water vessel *40*

PICTURE CREDITS

Alamy: 11 (North Wind/Nancy Carter), 19 (Andrew Molinaro), 20 (Jim West), 23 bottom (ED Images), 24 (North Wind/Nancy Carter), 31 top (David Wei), 32 (North Wind/Nancy Carter), 34 (Interfoto), 39 (Mireille Vautier), 45 (National Geographic/W Langdon Kihn), 48 (Chronicle), 51 (Interfoto/Travel), 52 (Francesco Abrignani), 53 (Chronicle), 55 & 58 (Danita Delimont/Angel Wynn), 59 (Art Collection 2), 64 (Danita Delimont/Angel Wynn), 66 (Paul Long), 72 (AGE Fotostock/George Ostertag), 75 (Leon Werdinger), 79 top (Mireille Vautier), 82 (Chuck Place), 84 (Lebrecht), 86 (Chuck Place), 88 (Chronicle), 93 (Luc Novovitch), 103 (Danita Delimont/Angel Wynn), 112 (AGE Fotostock/Alan Majchrowicz), 113 (Classic Image), 114 (Science History Images), 118 (Glasshouse Images/J T Vintage), 121 & 122 (North Wind), 123 (Atomic), 129 (Lee Rentz), 133 (NSF), 136 (Buddy Mays), 138 (Interfoto), 146 (Hemis/Philippe Renault), 149 (William Brooks), 150 (United Archives), 157 (National Geographic/W Langdon Kihn), 158 (Rick & Nora Bowers), 160 (Cayman), 163 (Chronicle), 164 (Classic Stock/H Armstrong Roberts), 168 (North Wind), 172 (Archive PL), 178 (World History Archive), 183 (Chronicle), 190 & 191 (David Wei), 194 (Niday Picture Library), 199 (Kuco), 205 (Interfoto), 210 (Classic Stock/H Armstrong Roberts), 213 (Classic Stock/H Armstrong Roberts), 214 (North Wind), 217 (George Ostertag), 218 (Danita Delimont/Angel Wynn), 220 (WHA/Desmond Morris Collection)

Alamy/Granger Collection: 6, 8, 25, 31 bottom, 47, 87, 94, 102, 110, 119, 137, 141 bottom, 145, 169, 175, 177, 179, 192, 196

Alamy/HIP/Werner Forman: 7, 23 top, 63 bottom, 120, 141 top, 151, 170, 212 both

J B Illustrations © Amber Books: 29, 106, 140, 153, 197

Bridgeman Art Library: 77 (Butler Institute of American Art), 100 (Look & Learn), 176 (Stapleton Collection)

Dreamstime: 162 (Maryanne Perrier)

Mary Evans Picture Library: 109 (Everett Collection)

Getty Images: 22 (Dorling Kindersley), 28 (Corbis/Library of Congress), 38 (Corbis/Marilyn Angel Wynn), 40 (Hulton), 44 (Corbis/Marilyn Angel Wynn), 65 (Corbis/Library of Congress), 68 (Bettmann), 80 (Popperfoto), 83 (Nativestock/Marilyn Angel Wynn), 104 & 107 (Corbis), 134 (Superstock/Jerome Kleine), 159 (Portland Press Herald), 174 (UIG/Photo12), 184/185 (Hulton/Apic), 187 (Corbis/Historical PictureArchive), 203 (Archive Photos/MPL), 209 (Corbis)

Getty Images/Universal Images Group/Werner Forman: 21, 30, 41, 78, 85, 91 top, 139, 144

Library of Congress: 10, 14, 16, 18, 27, 33, 36, 42, 56/57, 60, 62, 63 top, 67, 69, 73, 74, 89, 91 bottom, 92, 97, 108, 111, 124/125, 126, 130, 131, 132, 142/143, 152, 154/155, 166/167, 171 both, 181, 182, 188, 189, 198, 201, 202, 204, 206/207, 216

Shutterstock: 13 (The Black Rhino), 70 (Keri in the Wild), 98/99 (Eric Backman), 147 (Claudette Cormier), 193 (C Clair), 200 (Visionteller)